Sanctuary Dishonored

The Decline and Fall of the Maxfield Parrish Estate

ROBIN LEE

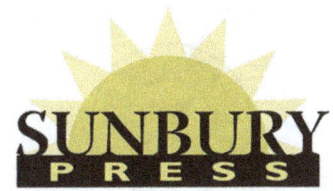

SUNBURY PRESS

Mechanicsburg, Pennsylvania   USA

Published by Sunbury Press, Inc.
50 West Main Street, Suite A
Mechanicsburg, Pennsylvania 17055

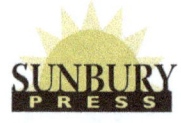

www.sunburypress.com

For information about special discounts for bulk purchases, please contact Sunbury Press Orders Dept. at (855) 338-8359 or orders@sunburypress.com.

To request one of our authors for speaking engagements or book signings, please contact Sunbury Press Publicity Dept. at publicity@sunburypress.com.

ISBN: 978-1-62006-362-0 (Trade Paperback)
ISBN: 978-1-62006-363-7 (Hard Cover)

FIRST SUNBURY PRESS EDITION: May 2014

Product of the United States of America
0 1 1 2 3 5 8 13 21 34 55

Set in Bookman Old Style
Designed by Lawrence Knorr
Cover by Lawrence Knorr
Edited by Lawrence Knorr

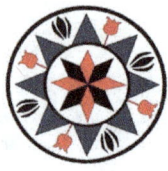

Continue the Enlightenment!

Dedication

I dedicate this book to my children Toby, Calah, Kory, and Chantal. You are so very precious to me and I love you all so much. You are my blessings, you are my heartbeat.

To my dad, Donald M., I love you.

To my mom and my grandparents, I miss you.

To all of the struggling artists, believe in yourself, have faith, pray, and give thanks.

To all of those reading my book, thank you. Volunteer whenever and wherever you can and always count your blessings. Be kind to animals everywhere!

Acknowledgments

Brenda M. – A true Christian friend who was always there, helping me to get this book published - you are my best friend

Seth B. – For believing in this project and bringing your talents to the table

Kirsten C. – For pulling me back and watching for red flags

Johanna M. – For your brilliance - you rock

Linda V. – My bud, for being wise and so lovely

Mark R. – For your wisdom and prayers

Frank K. – For being a true friend - marvelous

Matt N. - For being the best audience ever

Peg M. – For your prayers and kindness

Kaja – For your excellent guidance

Mark D. – For being Editor of the Year

Sunbury Press – For discovering me

Marla M. – For helping me with this puzzle

Foreword

Born in Philadelphia, Pennsylvania, Maxfield Parrish was the son of painter and etcher Stephen Parrish. His given name was Frederick Parrish but he later adopted the maiden name of his paternal grandmother, Maxfield, as his middle name, and later as his professional name. He began drawing for his own amusement as a child, and Parrish's young parents encouraged his talent. He later attended Haverford College, the Pennsylvania Academy of the Fine Arts, and Drexel Institute of Art, Science & Industry. He entered into an artistic career that lasted for more than half a century, and which helped shape the Golden Age of illustration and the future of American visual arts. He was one of the most successful and prolific of the illustrators and painters of the Golden Age of Illustration. He was earning over $100,000 per year by 1910, at a time when a fine home could be purchased for $2,000. Norman Rockwell referred to Parrish as "my idol." Parrish, although unique in his execution and never duplicated, exhibited considerable influence upon other illustrators and artists, an influence which continues through the present. His original paintings are highly sought-after when they come to market, as well as his first-edition prints, which continue to command high prices at both auction and through private sales. His exacting attention to detail preceded the Photorealist and Hyper-Realist art movements, and his abundant imagination and love of fantasy elements have also influenced artists in myriad media.[1]

---

1 Maxfield Parrish, www.Wikipedia.org, Retrieved January 24, 2014

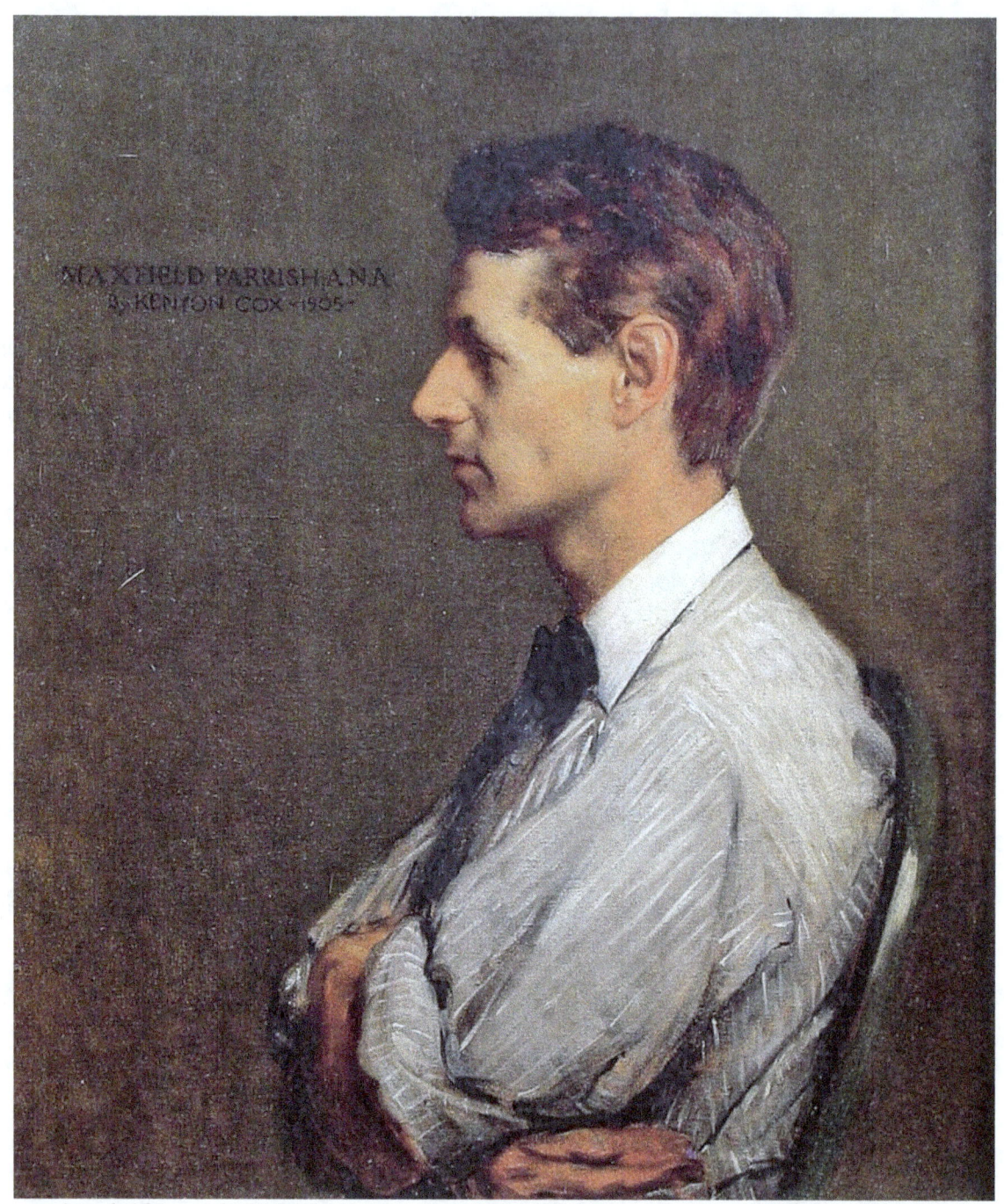

Maxfield Parrish (1905) by Kenyon Cox (1856-1919), Oil on canvas, 30" x 25", National Academy Museum (New York, United States)

Introduction

Dreamland—my thoughts—a journey—an event. It all came together throughout a twenty-year run. In the early 1990s, something outrageously sweet entered into my life; I was at the estate of the late Maxfield Parrish, the world famous artist. What I witnessed there—what took place—should infuriate you.

I hope that you will not just read this story, but feel it. Maybe some odd shivers will start around the base of your neck. Maybe it will become a little difficult to breathe or take in a deep breath, as though your chest is tight. All is well. A hovering sense—a delightful sensation—polite quivers—passionate outbursts in a yearning to increase both sorrow and joy—a symphony of music. You may hear art history forever gone. Plenty of emotions will surface in different ways, and all are worthy of opinions. Come to your own conclusions—explore what you may not understand—magnify your inner thoughts.

If pictures are worth a million words, these millions of words seem elusive to me— stolen dreams from all of us—a harvest of innocence—a surrendering to betrayal. It is punishment: naked, excavated, rearranged, transformed without meaning—broken, buried, a rootless existence, a violation everlasting.

To create art is to love and to love is art. It seems the art that we create is a true reflection of who we are. It can be as plain as the nose on your face. As I wrote this manuscript I did not write it alone. There was someone else here. And his words, his emotions, were woven in with mine. Can you feel the shivers up your spine? You will. *Enter dreamland—proceed ahead, steadfast and faithfully.*

Robin's Tale

An old New England story with all of its charm is about to unfold. I will be as honest as I can and ask you to allow yourself a clear mind so that you can better understand. It was 1993 and I was living up in the White Mountains of New Hampshire. I'm a musician, a flautist. I play other instruments, but flute is my passion. I had begun composing music in my little recording studio built off the side of my home, overlooking hills and dales. I decorated the walls of my studio with enchanting posters by an artist, Maxfield Parrish. For some reason, I became obsessed with this artist, buying all of the books about him and vintage prints of his work. Soon, the walls of my home were covered in Parrish prints, and at auctions, I would bid on every Parrish I could find. These prints became my inspiration when composing and recording music. I never used sheet music when recording and I never wrote anything down. I used those beautiful prints by Parrish as my sheet music to create my first CD, entering into a painting and creating the music to fit into it. I had a gift, as I could play by ear, and it became easy to let myself go, like a child, inside his paintings.

When that first CD was completed, I used a Parrish print as the front cover. The CD looked and sounded perfect. I sent the CD out to many music magazines. After learning that the Parrish estate was here in New Hampshire, near me, I decided to send a CD to one of the owners of the Parrish estate. The music magazines sent me excellent reviews on my music and praised my connection with Parrish and my work. I did not receive one bad review! During this time, I also had a phone call from a part owner of the Parrish estate asking if I'd like to come over to have tea with her. How exciting! Imagine how I felt, being invited to tea at the historical estate of the late Maxfield Parrish! This was a dream come true; a combination of so many emotions came sensuously over me, disassembling me. At the same time, I felt something else beckoning me, pulling me, calling out to me. I would soon find out what that was...

It was a warm, breezy, sunny day as I drove to the Parrish estate to have tea with my hostess. I had chills chasing up and down my spine, looking over the map for the quickest way to get there. Before I knew it I was turning up a road—called Freeman

2

Road—his road—climbing a large hill. He traveled up and down this very same road! I took a photo of an old handmade sign and proceeded. Then, there it was—on the right— the beginning of the entrance-way leading up to his studio. A pair of wrought iron gates welcomed me. They were swung open—craftily designed—old and glorious.

The long, gracious driveway swirled up and around. Nearby sat an old red wagon off to the side. I'll bet it was his. I took a photo of that old red wagon. I loved it. My heart started pounding; my breathing became loud and heavy. *Embroidered songs weaving all around me; intensified themes, anxious, shaking, quivering, dewy eyes, silence and love.* Wow! That's what you go through entering onto his grounds, or at least that's what I went through. It felt really good, like a first kiss. I adored this feeling. Where did it come from?

I pulled my car around to a parking spot in front of two gigantic oak trees. I had read about these two trees—they were centuries old. Parrish loved them so much that he called his estate The Oaks. There they towered—handsome—huge—massive trunks— begging for attention. They had long, thick limbs that warmly reached out to me— showing off—proud.

The grounds—the landscape—I felt like I was in a dream where I could fly. I had flown over these grounds many times throughout my life—the horticulture—the division of space—stonewalls coming and going wherever they wanted to go—stone archways— old trees—shrubs—a progression and sloping of his lawns—contoured—intertwining into each other. I heard soft meaningless words—polite whispers—vague and passionate.

The gardens were full of sweet, scented air and were overgrown, but colorful, with flowers mirrored in the morning dew. Herbaceous plants were found in the foreground behind ancient stone walls along with generations of indigenous plants.

It was a mid-summer night's dream. I was waiting for pixies, brownies, and fairies to emerge out of their hiding places. I felt as if I were in a fairy tale—a palette of colors dancing all around me in harmony. Such a performance! I heard whispers of an old language behind me, but no one was there. The breeze was picking up and blew my hair all around my face and it felt good. *Give me unquiet dreams to take back with me.* Who was holding my hand?

My hostess comes over to greet me. She was warm, polite and educated. She was tiny with large eyes and a welcoming smile. She was very well-dressed and gracious, her presence demanding. As we stood there, she began telling me all about the estate, pointing to the buildings and stonewalls. She knew the history very well, and had much to say. She had owned many Parrish paintings and had also written books about him. I was in good hands. I was thrilled to be there!

We started to walk down an old stone stairway to the main house. A fire had destroyed the original home that Parrish built decades ago and a new home was built in its place. There were endless views in the front of the home, and in the middle of that lawn, there was a round reflecting pool with a fountain. I had seen that pool and that view in his paintings. They were unmistakable. In fact, many of the stone walls, archways, trees, and gardens were in many of his paintings. It was everywhere you looked, and I knew his paintings well. They were infused with his former property.

My host and I had a wonderful tea together and she showed me all around.

My camera was clicking away at all the beauty that surrounded me. We went to the upper level of the home where his main studio was. She was talking, pointing out this and that, but I was wandering off in thought—admiring this property—sleeping—poetic—a devotion to his paintings—youthful and ageless. We exited the house and began to walk down a pathway that led to acres of lush green grass accompanied by high stone archways, which were falling apart.

I wanted to take off my shoes and run like a carefree girl—chase me—catch me if you can—tag, you're it!--come find me—running in and out of his paintings. All the while, my gaze kept fixating on his art studio, the place where I really wanted to go.

The afternoon passed and I did not want to wear out my welcome. I was invited back again and again. I would be back. As I left, I looked at his art studio—how historic it looked—but what did it look like inside? During my next visit, I would be allowed that privilege and honor.

All the way home, these elegant classical melodies sang to me. Once home, I composed and recorded those melodies—those little masterpieces. I began to write a journal about my visit to the Parrish estate and all I had encountered. I was glad to have taken so many photos. The estate lingered with me. I could still smell it and feel it. I could hear the whispers. It wrapped itself all around me like a blanket.

I accepted the invitation to return to the Parrish estate, but this time I went with camcorder in hand in order to film the secret inside world of Parrish's art studio. As I approached the gates on Freeman Road, my body started tingling all over. As I went through those wrought iron gates, an intense, pleasant feeling came over me again—delightfully complicated—consuming and overwhelming. My hostess greeted me with a smile. I was happy to be there. It was another beautiful day which brought great weather. The sun was shining, and the breeze once again brought all of the floral scents from the flowers to play with my nose.

During this visit I was allowed the privilege to enter Parrish's art studio. There it stood—long—old—grand—historic and very weathered. It was a large building with many windows, and on the lower level, connected by an oblong cement pond--a reflecting pool overgrown with plants—cracked—dissolving—broken and neglected. It had three old archways next to it, most likely connecting it to the basement of the massive art studio.

How clearly I was able see those archways and that pool in many of his paintings. They had a European look to them. It was sad to see how they had been let go, to fall into such disrepair.

The Parrish studio had a powerful pull to it—pure—old and gay—surviving the decades—strong—formal—symmetrical and dominating. It had been designed and constructed well by Parrish—the artist and his studio—mature detailing—creative.

I stood in front of the studio entranceway. There was an old, red, three-paneled door with and old brass doorknocker embedded into it. It was the very same red as that old wagon at the end of his driveway that I saw during my first visit.

There were two old lamps hanging on each side of his entranceway next to swirling wrought-iron brackets, and the overhang above was a simple copper roof. As I was about to walk through and touch the old doorknob he used, I leaned over and thought to myself, "Guess who?" I was on hallowed grounds—sacred—surviving—waiting.

I opened the door and crossed over into his inner world. Whispers breathed into my hand—a rush came over me. I felt weepy—anxious—floating—as I looked around. The hostess guided me, explaining all that I was viewing and touching. I could not feel my feet. I was not touching the floor. I was there in his studio, where he had been. It was magnificent—no words—sensations—soaring. I couldn't hear a word she was saying. I was hopelessly in love—breathe—focus.

We entered the large main room—tall ceilings—an old man scent—strong—fragile. This room had a *Romeo and Juliet* balcony in it—way up there with this round motif. I had seen this motif in his other rooms. It must have been his motif.

The *Romeo and Juliet* balcony was so Shakespeare—so romantic. It had a little secret stairway to get up to it. In fact, there were other secret passageways around his studio. I went up this narrow little creaking stairway—up in the balcony I stood—so Juliet. How odd and yet wonderful it was to have such a balcony in one's home.

Similar to his playful grounds, rooms were intertwining with each other—playing—flowing into each other. What a wonderful world in there! It was warm and inviting, and had that great New England look and feel to it.

The arts and crafts period was 1860 to 1925. Such craftsmanship—outstanding—of days gone by—and I felt privileged to be there. Parrish built and designed this with such texture and architectural precision—his castle—home to a romantic visionary. There were built-ins, including the large fireplace by which he warmed himself. A noble, delightful image was surrounding me, making me humbled and appreciated.

We walked out to a balcony, enclosed in ivy-clad, wrought-iron railings, where I was told he would have his afternoon tea.

The New England birds were singing to us and, to understand how perfect it was to be here, imagining him sitting—sipping tea—inspiration coming at him from all these glorious views. These views were all there in his paintings—all of them. We then went into the room on the very end of his studio—a very sunny room with large windows. This room had a large, sliding garage door built in on one wall which he used that to bring out large paintings and panels that would not fit through the other doorways. This room, like several others, was cluttered and messy with carpenter tools, saws, and the like, which made it difficult to move around. I asked my hostess why things were in such a state of disarray at the estate to which she informed me that there was intent by the main owner to convert it into condos and or a new home. I was appalled to hear this. It was so difficult to see his place being destroyed and not preserved. I wanted to protect it, but how?

All I could think about was how I'd love to come back here with my instruments and equipment and record music. I thought if he could be inspired here, maybe I could too. I also wanted to take my photos while I could—as many as I'd be allowed. My hostess thought that this was a wonderful idea, to try and be inspired by the very same inspirations that Parrish painted. Somehow I felt that this was why I was there. I felt a warmth take over me, a sense of stillness and timelessness, with a hint of reassurance.

We came out another entranceway—an entrance grander than that of the studio, with two fine white columns on each side of the doorway. It was elegant and formal and I had seen these columns in one of his most famous paintings, *Daybreak*. To the side of his studio near that room with the garage door was an outhouse, a double-decker with two potties in it, still useable.

Down on the lower level of the lawn was an old stone archway situated in the middle of a fine stone masonry wall. Although the archway was still standing, one could see that the New England weather gave it a run for the money and erosion was taking over. What was peculiar about this archway was all of the wine bottles which were protruding from the masonry. There were lots of them—old brown and green vintage wine bottles—unbroken—placed there by the masonry workers during their lunch break so long ago.

My hostess told me that they probably drank during lunchtime and hid the bottles in their work.

The entire estate was in great need of repair and restoration as it had been neglected for such a long time. I was still in shock that his art studio was being transformed into something else. It should be preserved and kept to its original condition, 100%. This estate was his canvas and it was precious—a gift for all of us. It is a historic place—the home of a great artist. It was hard to leave. The ride back home was long—recalling how his studio was about to be ruined. I didn't understand. What could I do?

Back at home in the White Mountains, I began going through all of my Maxfield Parrish books. Where I had been that day—his estate—the views—the gardens—and his studio—were in every painting. I wrote in my Parrish journal of the day's events—made sure to cover every detail—every emotion—and every odd event that happened. I couldn't wait to go back there—how restless I was. I was in love with his estate.

Twas another fine day in Ye Olde New England: great weather, sunshine, birds singing. I loaded up the car with instruments, video camera, and more. I was ready to record and compose music at the estate of Maxfield Parrish. Off I went to the land of make believe. *Look Out.*

As I approached the entranceway framed by the open gates, I felt a presence awaiting me—inviting me. Each time I would arrive at the site, I would become emotional—my heart pounding—my eyes becoming dewy. My goodness—such drama, such excitement!

My hostess greeted me and we exchanged happy hugs. She helped me unload my musical instruments and we proceeded into his studio. Shivers took over me as I floated out to his balcony. All those dreamy views are waiting, creative heirlooms on canvas I'll try to capture through my compositions. I took out my flute, set up, and just let myself go. I closed my eyes and played. I was gone.

It was like a scene from a movie. I was driven. I was in his world—paddling in shadows—playing my flute with conflict and the playing taking over—beautiful—bold melodies. Where were they all coming from? I was effortlessly composing one mesmerizing song after another. Wonderful, consuming emotions were taking over—they were everywhere. Emotions, both good and bad, are a composer's best friend. This estate was heavy with them—they were endless—gifts of love—love that gives. These compositions were full and heavy with joy and peace—a faithfulness of beauty flourishing into my flute. *Let love be genuine and live in harmony. Let the wellspring of wisdom take over. Sorrow we will all share; it should remain changeless.* What I did not understand as I composed was devouring me in rivers of woe. *Somber wounded heart linger longer so that I may get a glimpse of you as these wondrous songs are born. Arms of love, yearning, appear grateful. Love doth be a friend like a wondering soul. Nourish this presence and breathe into my hand. How I love every melody I compose and the others will go into hiding, dormant until a later time.* What just happened? How delightful!

I went inside his studio to find another sweet spot where I could feel his presence the most. Flute in hand, I began to play more skillfully, intensely. *Void of meaning, distress was present in this anguished fortress. Images restrained, trembling in a dark veil; a perfection of beauty here in his art studio. These melodies receive distress, sorrow's tears, a cruel vision, wreckage to consume his paradise. I'm glad I'm recording this...***Sanctuary dishonored?**

It was a strange way to compose music, but it worked for me. I was connecting to more than this music--I was connecting to a wounded heart in the midst of helplessness. I was embraced—humbled—content in grief—hidden in the depths of emptiness—shadowed. So much passion engulfed that room that one could climb the air. I was grateful. I felt as though I was in a dream. I was rejoicing in my glorious compositions, yet I was somehow consoled and was bathed in the warm sunlight that streamed through a window. Songs! More songs were embedded deep inside of me, imprinted forever, like a storm preserved in time.

Alleluia, such an experience and accomplish-ment—triumphant airy cast-les appear in haze. I celeb-rate quietly in another time and place and realize where I am—focused to get back. Consuming passion with mercy, imperceptible illusion, and fractured cracks in a collision with time and ignorance, yet the song becomes the strength and all is quiet.

Decades later these compositions would be recorded. My journal, my music, and my notes will be well hidden until then. I thought to myself, when the time is right, the best songs will then be released. All in good time, all for good reason. Patience.

Back at home in the White Mountains, I began to piece my compositions together in my recording studio. I decided which songs to release on the next two CDs, while the others, those that are special and must wait, although I did not know why, go under lock and key. I also wrote down every detail of my last visit in my journal. It turned out that those next two Parrish-inspired CDs were released close together and were very well received by the media, newspapers, local television, and magazines. Even A.P. Network news came out to cover the Parrish story! All loved the Parrish connection and inspiration. Music reviews in magazines were excellent – all of them. Soon famous people, musicians, and composers wrote, called or faxed, asking questions and giving advice, trying to steal what I had. "Sign here so we can take control of your music and story." I signed nothing. I knew what I had, and with all the attention I was getting, I had a good idea that this was just the beginning. Proceed with caution I said to myself. Protect the panel and wait for the right time and place.

It was now autumn in New England, such a display of colors and droves of tourists. It's my favorite season. The air is always delicious with a potent woodsy smell. I was on my way to the Parrish estate, anticipating the view from that hill with miles of colorful vistas. It was also harvest time and there's plenty of roadside stands on the way with bountiful displays of vegetables; pumpkins, squash, apples, mums, cider and homemade country baked goods, still warm. I stopped to buy some goodies for my hostess.

I was lost in thought and anticipation as I made the drive to the Parrish property. I was on a quest to validate the importance of his artwork and his inspiration with my music. What an amazing honor for me. Finally I was approaching Freeman Road. Through those old gates I went, past that poor old red wagon, still standing there, waiting. Parrish must have had a lot of fun with that wagon. I wondered to myself why it had not been carefully stored and had instead been left out to ruin in the weather? I parked my car up between those two big poets, the oak trees. *Hello!* Then I froze.

In sorrow and in disbelief I could see the front of Parrish's beloved art studio pulled apart, exposed. That perfect entranceway with the great old red door and lanterns was gone! The other, more elegant, entrance with those two white columns was gone! So many piles of broken boards, doors, windows, walls, and fixtures—all waiting to be taken away and discarded forever.

They were like a trail of diamonds, all glittering, but helpless. Pieces of the exterior and interior were blanketed all over the lawn. I could see what was left of that old copper roof hood that hung over the first entrance.

In a pile of precious junk, one of the unbroken white columns yelled out to me. I pulled it out carefully and gave it to my hostess. We both stood there like two beaten stones. I went from pile to pile in order to recognize every piece of his studio which should be honored and remembered. This was a historic landmark! I was in shock. All of those piles of history—and love—the architectural front—now in piles of rubbish! All should remain as he created it, preserved, protected and restored to its original condition. I went down an embankment overgrown with saplings, trees, vines and creepers. It was such a profusion of overgrowth, tranquil, lost in time. This was the rear of the property that had not yet been touched. It too stood there helpless, waiting its turn—paradise.

My hostess and I went back to the front of the property and went inside his studio. It was a mess, pulled apart, all of the delicate details ruined. I stood there sad and bewildered. My hostess took me down to his basement, which I had not yet visited. It was all untouched—his tools—toys—and mechanisms (pulleys, wheels and gears) of all kinds. What a place to create and build! There were all types of craftsman items that were most likely used to create much of this home. I could only imagine Parrish in this machine shop, building, creating, fixing, playing, and doing what artists love to do. I began to record a video in this room. I truly enjoyed this room that was full of his creativity and seemed to hold a sense of him being here working. I could picture him making all of the old birdhouses which were on the property, building frames, panels, and making props for his paintings.

My hostess and I walked back out and again, standing there like two beaten stones frozen and bewildered. We pointed to those piles of estate, broken but recognizable archives, destroyed and torn from their place, waiting to be discarded and forgotten.

But wait. I noticed a perfectly preserved, green painted panel with that same, circular protruding motif that I had seen inside his art studio, like the much larger one that was under the Romeo and Juliet balcony. I wanted this smaller green one. Somehow I felt it was speaking to me, but I was not about to divulge that secret. My hostess allowed me that panel. I was not about to let it be discarded into a landfill! I held it in my hands like an old treasure—an heirloom—as if it were waiting and familiar to me. *"I had this premonition about you", I said to it. "Yes I know. I'm glad you listened."*

I couldn't wait to get this panel home—my Parrish panel. It was exquisite—steeped in history and sublime beauty. Oh how I was drawn to it—its rare—aged—insightful artistic beauty. I then whisked it off to my car, wrapped it in a blanket, and secured it with a seat belt.

There was always something else at that estate hovering over my head—a delicate shy existence—like someone was trying to tell me a secret and having a hard time expressing it. It was difficult to leave. I didn't think I would go back. Secrets would just have to wait for another time and place. His oak trees waved goodbye, the wind was picking up and I glanced back for one last look at what they had done to his studio and all old that lay broken on his lawn. Such an historic place, stupid, naked, ignorance.

This was a place for scholars, poets
And artists long after we're gone.

The estate was a unique landmark that should have been left in its original condition, 100% perfect, Parrish-made condition. Every aspect of it, every door, every board, every nail, every doorknob, every window he looked out, should have been cherished and not thrown away.

Sometimes, I think I did not come home alone that day. I was told Parrish was laid to rest just a few minutes down the road and I realized that I had to go and see his gravesite. As the native New Englander Steven King says, "They tell a story, the cemetery."

The Plainfield Cemetery, where Maxfield Parrish is buried, is located off the beaten path. The only indication of the cemetery was a lonely, leaning, crooked sign, marking the entrance. There was a long, well-built, hand-made, stonewall with two tall columns on each side of the cemetery entrance. A fine representation of good ole New England workmanship surviving the centuries. There was nothing that signified that Maxfield Parrish was laid to rest behind the impressive entrance.

It was a typical 1800s to 1900s New England cemetery—thick colorful moss carpets under dry crackling autumn leaves. An orange setting sun filtered through the trees resting upon random headstones. The smell of the cemetery and autumn was all around. It was quaint, quiet, lonely, and haunting, and like every old New England cemetery, owned by ravens or crows. As I walked into his cemetery, the crows began their loud, orchestrated discord at me. I was uninvited and unfamiliar to them and they wanted me gone. But I admired them and they had my respect. They possessed such strong family and social ties; devoted and brilliant. They surveyed the cemetery, watching me, all the while recording and imprinting. One bird stood up high, perched on the tallest headstone, cawing repeatedly, up and down, up and down, and then stopped. He was like an art nouveau sculpture—satin black. Two others perched way up high, in two, almost leafless maples, which stood symmetrically like two Parrish stencils. Watching the birds was a good diversion for me—refreshing. I replied to every question they asked. They were so very nosy. They flew from tree to tree, shining like jet black glassware, with hints of shimmering blue hues in their feathers. They emerged from distant trees and asked, "Who's in our cemetery?" They all listened to my hushed reply, as I have a way with birds—these beautiful birds with their armor of black stained glass against a setting sun. A perfume of burning wood in the autumn air rose. I knew twilight was near and I preferred to not drive in the dark on these New England back roads with deer crossing signs every two miles.

I hurriedly began to search the cemetery for Parrish's headstone to beat the impending twilight, all the while the crows continued to monitor me, curiously, with their black porcelain armor, expressive yet comforting. I wished I had some bread with me to placate them. It did not take me long to find the Master's final resting place.

"Oh there you are!" I thought to myself as I saw a small, plain, flat granite stone embedded in the earth.

Maxfield Parrish
1870-1966

Next to Parrish rested his son, another flat stone, the same as Parrish's. He was a young man when he passed.

John Dillwyn Parrish
1904-1959

There was no sign of Parrish's wife's resting place. She had left him to his precious work in his studio with his lovely, flawless model, Sue Lewin, long ago. Sue was not his mistress, but simply his model and she was very present in so many of his most famous pieces. He'd not only dress Sue for the innocent beautiful lady, but he used her as his male models, mostly young men, late teens, early twenties, sensuous, sexual. She was both male and female, youthful and playful. She was his work of art—innocent. She was many things to him but she was never a mistress—never a lover. I assumed the town gossip discussed otherwise, and could only assume that Parrish's wife was aware of his lifestyle. His paintings reflected this dichotomy and elicited the question of "what else may have been going on?"

I found it odd that close to Parrish's final resting place lie Sue Lewin. Sue Lewin had married her childhood sweetheart around the age of 70!

Susan L. Colby
1889, 1970, Wife of Earle W. Colby

It was sad, and rather odd, to see no homage to Parrish attributed to her gravesite. I thought back to what kind of rumbling town gossip Parrish and his family had to endure. It would have been safer for them to assume Sue as his mistress. What Parrish must have endured personally and what he carried on his shoulders must have been an inspiration for his paintbrush! An old New England town, juicy with gossip—can you imagine Parrish, maybe Sue in tow, going to the Town Store? Oh, to have been a fly on the wall and to have heard the scream of the torched flame thrown at them by the town folk! My heart went out to Parrish, trying to survive in a time of such misunderstanding. How such a secret, a sweet secret, probably impacted all those magnificent paintings? How he created—how he saw—how beautiful—how so very beautiful. Parrish. Cemeteries do tell a story. Oh yes. This cemetery was a book, volume one.

I completed my Parrish journal, hung that panel on my wall, and hid the gate spokes and frame. How thankful I was to have been there at that exact point in time, but why was I there?

In 2008, I left New Hampshire with my daughter and ended up on the coast of Maine. It is a warm, coastal village with a fabulous harbor, a place where the mountains meet the sea. This coast is filled with kind people and had become a sort of Mecca for many talented artists and musicians. My daughter and I had so much fun discovering this coastal bliss, swimming in the lake, beachcombing, and just enjoying being together and happy. There were yard sales, concerts, festivals, art openings, castles, boats, and even a library three floors high overlooking the peaceful harbor and out to sea. Christmas time reminded me of a Norman Rockwell painting—an enchanted winter wonderland. Christmas by the sea, locals and tourists all mingling and enjoying the festivities. The village shops were beautifully decorated, with cookies and mulled cider on the tables. I was on cloud nine, my world was glowing; both my daughter and I were content, fixing up our new home, making good new friends. All was well. We had found sanctuary.

After an unfortunate turn of events, my daughter had to move back to New Hampshire. I found myself lost without her. I began to lose trust in everything and my heart was broken. My health began to decline. As winter continued, something strange had begun to happen. The panel from the Parrish estate had a hum to it, attracting me to it, whispering. I could swear the panel was trying to communicate with me. I would hold it and my skin would tingle, my insides would tighten, my hair would stand up, and the room would go cold. I would begin to sense an overwhelming presence, a very strong, very demanding presence.

Out of curiosity, I took the panel to an auctioneer whom I knew was honest. I also brought all of my photos, videos, and other archives from the Parrish estate. He was amazed at what I had to show him and encouraged me to promote my story anywhere I could. He gave me the names and addresses of contacts at three major magazine publishers with whom to follow through. He noted one magazine in particular of the three was the best. I decide to call this magazine, after much rehearsal.

To my surprise, I was connected directly with the Editor-in-Chief when I called the magazine! I composed myself and begin to talk about my journey to the Parrish estate and my consequent experiences. She listened to what I had to say, uninterrupted, and then asked a few questions. She had a kind, soft voice and we connected immediately. She asked that she be allowed to come visit from Boston to cover my story!

Once she had arrived, I showed her the photos I took of the estate. I had already sent her a copy of my journal, my three CDs, and many articles of my music and story, so she was already well informed upon her arrival. She looked at my book full of Parrish paintings and could see for herself the incredible connection between his paintings and his estate and the devastation of it, the lack of preservation and historic worth. She pieces everything together and we exchange thoughts.

I had yet to show her the panel. I was not sure if the panel will behave—but she wanted to see it. I had it in my bedroom—hidden. We both went into my bedroom to view the panel. I simply handed it to her and stepped aside. She admired it and as I predicted, she began to have an experience with it.

She seemed to understand what was going on—in her line of work, she had come across other similar pieces with historic significance and history. Almost unmoved, she recounted how she has encountered things like this before, although this one was different—bigger. In her travels she'd seen a lot and was somewhat familiar.

Those whispers were loud. Did she hear them? To hold the panel is a very personal, undeniable experience, unique to each person who holds it. It imprints on you, covers you like a warm blanket--holding you.

We had a great experience together. She told me that she would get this story into the magazine but would wait for the fall edition because it was the best. It was a bigger edition covering more of New England!

My mother, still young, had just passed away. My father, now alone, had moved to a warmer climate. I found myself on the phone begging my dad to move to Maine so we could keep an eye on each other. But, he did not want to leave the warmth and all of his new church friends. We stayed in touch by calling each other all of the time. He sent me boxes of my mom's jewelry—such fun costume jewelry—which I would most likely never wear. I had heard of this neat woman in town who owned a ladies' shop and who bought jewelry to resell. I picked out many nice pins, necklaces, bracelets and rings to keep for myself and my daughter, but I decided to take the rest to the ladies' shop.

I connected with this woman at her shop to offer her my mom's jewelry. She told me that my mother had great taste and decided to buy some of the jewelry. We had a nice time chatting and became friends—enjoying lunches and walks to get ice cream together. It was so nice to have a new friend! I soon found out that my new friend held a Ph.D. in Psychology—attending Harvard and the Boston School of Medicine. I also learned that she was well known in this area and very much loved. As more time passed and our friendship grew, I told her a little about Parrish and his estate, and finally, about the panel.

One night, when she stopped over at my place for a visit, I wanted her to hold the panel, because I thought, maybe, that she could make some sense of all that I have experienced during my involvement with all things Parrish. She was a brilliant person, so why not see if she could shed some light on the matter?

This was overwhelmingly delightful that someone else could feel what I have been feeling—sensing that a part of Parrish was in fact connected with the panel! I was no longer alone in this "other worldly event" any more. She became a believer that night and has been an integral part in giving me strength and confidence to write this book. I finally felt at peace to go forward with what I had to do, whatever it would be, wherever it would lead me. I'm was on a quest—a quest with the panel.

I knew that I needed to get this Parrish story out to the public, but I would need to seek help and information. The Maine coast is a wellspring of talent where I could find the assistance I needed. I began by visiting a local magazine company which also publishes books—mostly by locals—mostly Maine folk. The company published a popular magazine which I have read for years, so I felt an immediate connection. The magazine always featured great articles and photos of coastal Maine and all the fabulous local events.

I was able to talk with an editor in the books department. I decided to lay it out, showing him all I had and telling him about the Parrish estate. I left some material with him. He asked to look over all of it all and get back to me once he was finished.

When I was asked to return to the magazine company, the editor said that he and the other "top heads" got together to go over everything I had. He said they were all familiar with Maxfield Parrish and his work, but since it wasn't truly a Maine story, they would have to decline to publish my story. I persisted a little with him on the importance of this story, then thanked him for his time and left. I cried in my car and went home. He was right. It was not a Maine story... not yet. I began to realize that everything was happening for a reason. A closed door sends you to another door—a better door—a bigger door that may lead you to what it is that must be done. I dubbed this new adventure as The Maxfield Parrish Quest.

A local friend in one of my civic groups once told me that Maxfield Parrish and N.C. Wyeth were friends. I had never heard of this friendship. I was living in Wyeth country, but I'm from Parrish country. The two artists lived relatively near to each other. As I began to dig into this information, I seemed to be disturbing the sand on the bottom of a lake. I called up many so-called experts on Wyeth asking about the Wyeth-Parrish connection. One thing I learned was that they both studied in the same art school, under the same teacher. A very famous art teacher, Howard Pyle.

Around the same time, both Wyeth and Parrish were on the front covers of major magazines. The first time I went to a local Wyeth museum and began to study Wyeth's artwork—although I am not an art expert—looking at a Wyeth painting and then a painting by Parrish—I noticed how they were very similar—same technique—same color and blends—the powerful imprinting they both give to the viewer—all similar except for the subject matter. Wyeth created so many paintings of war—the military—guns—army —whereas Parrish painted exquisitely elegant, youthful ladies atop pastoral mountains amid beautiful scenery. His paintings were calm and tranquil, and he painted young, nude men with milky white skin, almost feminine in their qualities. Parrish effortlessly drew the observer in, pulling one into the heart of his paintings. Look deep into his paintings, and you can sense what he is trying to tell you. A secret? I felt I knew Parrish's secret. When I added up all of the details, it made sense. Others in the art world suspected all along but no one would directly say it. Back in those days, things were so different. Having a wife and family was the norm, and an easy cover. Parrish lived up in his studio while his wife and children remained down below in the main house. They left him alone—left him alone in his sanctuary with his true love: his paintings.

In my search for more answers, I was finally able to connect with another art historian whom I had been persistently trying to contact for six months. He was 93 and one of the most well-known in his field. I had told him of the Parrish estate and its demise. How sad he was to hear this—so sad it not only came over the phone but also into my heart. He hadn't heard about the estate and he couldn't believe it. He said, "Maxfield must be rolling over in his grave, the poor man." I replied, "You have no idea." He wanted me to tell him more but I was afraid to say much more because his soft, frail voice was quivering with sorrow for Parrish.

I decided to ask him if he was aware of any connection between Parrish and Wyeth. "No one has ever asked me that question," he said, followed by a long silence. Then he answered, "How could they have not known each other. It's quite possible that their paths would have crossed, but there is no documentation on it." He seemed puzzled. After more silence he said, "Let me think about this and I will get back to you."

His assistant got on the phone and said, "He needs to rest now." I liked him. That phone conversation was one of the most important calls I had made throughout my research. His voice and his words empowered me, putting more wind in my sails, and gave me answers.

I still continued to research, calling and writing anyone and everyone I felt could help with my research. I received many different opinions on the Parrish/Wyeth connection that began to line up in my mind. Many dead ends, many upset people, and yet some of the experts told me what they thought and felt. Some of it made sense. Many of those I contacted refused to talk with me or answer my letters. I seemed to have stirred up things and got the attention of the art world. During this same time, a rather bizarre event took place.

Out of nowhere, I had the urge to paint. I found myself in an art store, buying containers of paint, brushes, canvasses, and glaze. I started to create real paintings with depth, color, and imagination. I have no idea from where this desire or skill came. One art expert from a local gallery came to see my work and was impressed. Others who saw my paintings were asking why I didn't put them in an art gallery to sell. I wasn't ready for that. There would be a time and place when I would be eager to show off my subject matter—my passion. One thing that I had always noticed about Parrish was that he truly painted who he was—his feelings—his love—his passion—and his secrets.

For the last seven years, a truly wonderful event took place in Camden—the Camden International Film Festival. People came from all around the world to this event in our peaceful little coastal town. A Hollywood-like crowd descended upon Camden to discover or be discovered and to view new films. The town was filled with the likes of producers, directors, film makers, actors, newcomers—all the while with V.I.P. passes swinging around their necks. The locals went down to the village, sat on benches and watched all the glitz and glamour and excitement. But this year, I was going to be a part of the festivities. Thanks to my fairy godmother and a fairy godfather, I had a VIP pass hanging around my neck, hobnobbing at the parties and trying to pitch my movie on Parrish. I was just thrown in there with Parrish shoving me from behind!

After procuring a schedule, I began going from one event to another, talking to as many people as I could, learning and writing down all of the information. I grabbed every pamphlet or paper. I watched and listened. There were some pretty big A-listers at the festival, delegates from A & E, HBO, and Tribeca Films. There were delegates from foundations of all types, production companies, and so many great parties and receptions. These people were so unique, so alive, with every emotion and penny is on the table. I carefully began networking.

I was nervous going to all of those big events with all of the A-listers in attendance, but I was very confident with my movie and music score. I had the magazine article and Parrish on my side, and I soon found out that that magazine attracted lots of attention. I was better able to pitch my idea, my music, and the significance of this movie when people held that magazine article in their hand and read it. In fact, I was the only composer at the festival. I was starting to learn their language, picking up on it rather quickly like I already knew it. For the first time in my life, surrounded by all of these creative people, I felt I was in my element.

During the three days of networking at the festival, I learned all that I could about the film industry, the conferences, the production companies, film organizations, and the major funders and backers which helped fuel the industry. Soon it all became easy-- normal. I felt I was exactly where I was supposed to be—where dreams do come true, and coastal Maine, my home, was providing me with all the right tools.

Two film industry executives asked me to send them what I could when they got back to New York. I was actually doing my homework on them, being picky with whom I wanted to share my story. I tried not to be too eager, for all answers may not necessarily be found at this film festival. This just may be a stepping stone.

I was confident of the value of what I had in my possession and would not rush to sign anything or become too involved.

I happened to notice one man in particular who had been standing behind me. I was curiously drawn to him, because he seemed to have an essence that surrounded him. He was well dressed, just standing there, very still. At once I felt that familiar shove at my back to approach him to talk with him. I decide to go to him. The closer I get, the harder it was to breathe. Smoothly, I approached him, and he fixated immediately upon me like he was waiting. I quickly introduced myself to him and asked who he was and why he was there. He told me he was a small time film producer, and lived right here in Maine where his was trying to get his career going.

I begin to tell him of my odd adventures at the Parrish estate—my rare photos—the panel—the presence, whispers—and my music score. I was trying to condense my story so as not to bore him, but he listened intently. He was extremely professional, making no eye contact as he continued to lean in closer to me so he could listen better among the other goings on in the packed room.

After I finished, an easy, comfortable, quiet smile formed on his face, and he began pondering, looking up at the ceiling, his hand resting on his chin. Then, the wisest words I had heard throughout the entire film festival came out of his mouth. "The movie should be about the panel—the panel's point of view."

Since the film festival, I have received several phone calls from film industry delegates or their assistants, and they are interested in my story. They advised me to get a film trailer, or at least a manuscript or published book, so that they could better find the right backers.

So there I was, throughout the winter of 2011 to 2012, writing this manuscript. It was funny how once you start, you can't stop--it holds you firmly in its grip. I chose to hand write the manuscript because I felt closer to it that way. I would wake up in the middle of the night and turn on the lights to write or rewrite parts here and there. I would shut out the world and get busy. It was important to me to finish the manuscript quickly in order to get it into form where I could showcase all of those rare photos taken at the Parrish Estate in the 90's. I had never released those photos to the public. I have the only copies. This is history and art. Both provide insight, information, and a story for you to judge. It is vital to acknowledge what has taken place; it raises many questions, yet answers others.

Let this story help to recharge the world of Maxfield Parrish—his life—his loves—who he was—who he is; a gift.

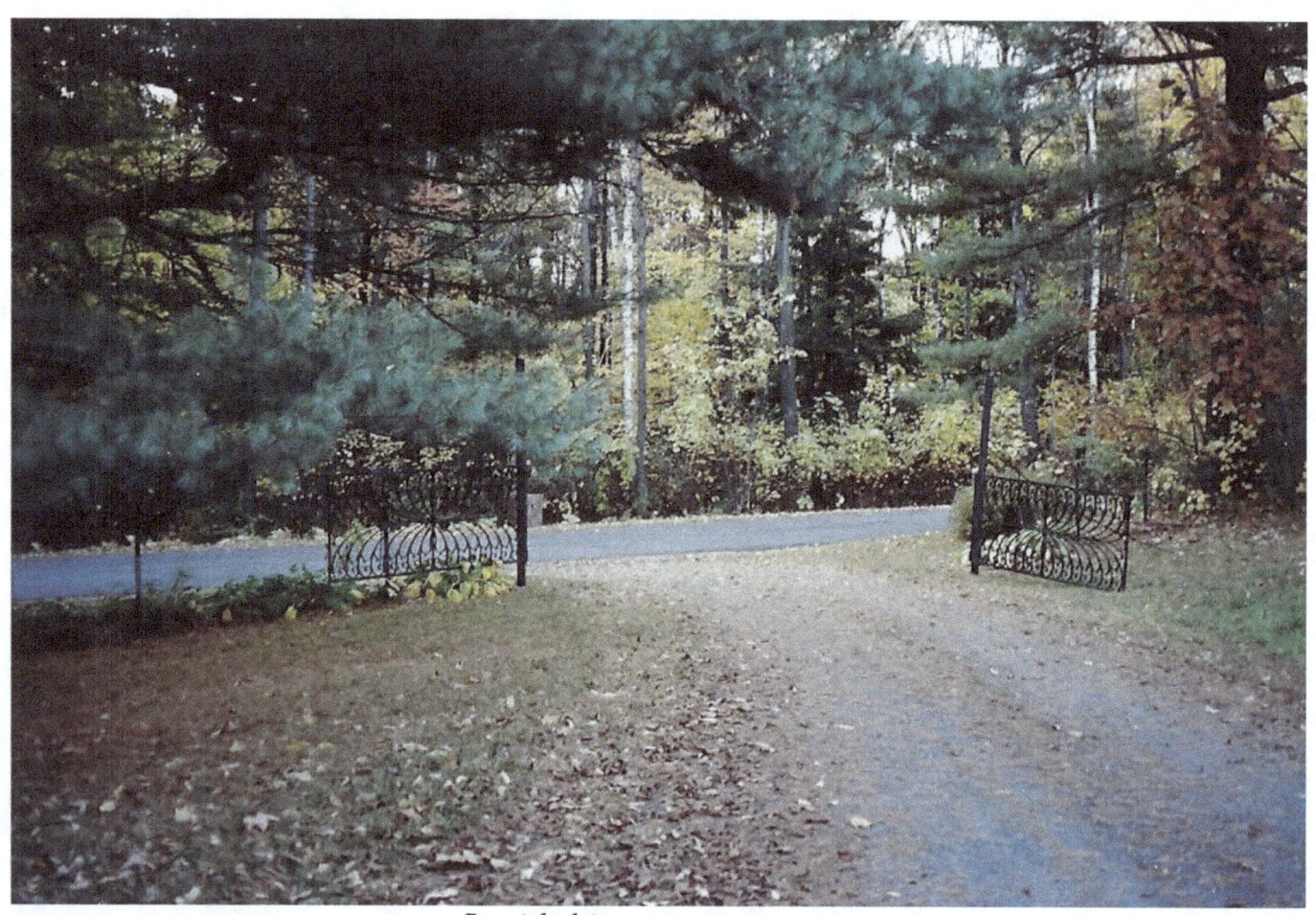

Parrish driveway entrance gate

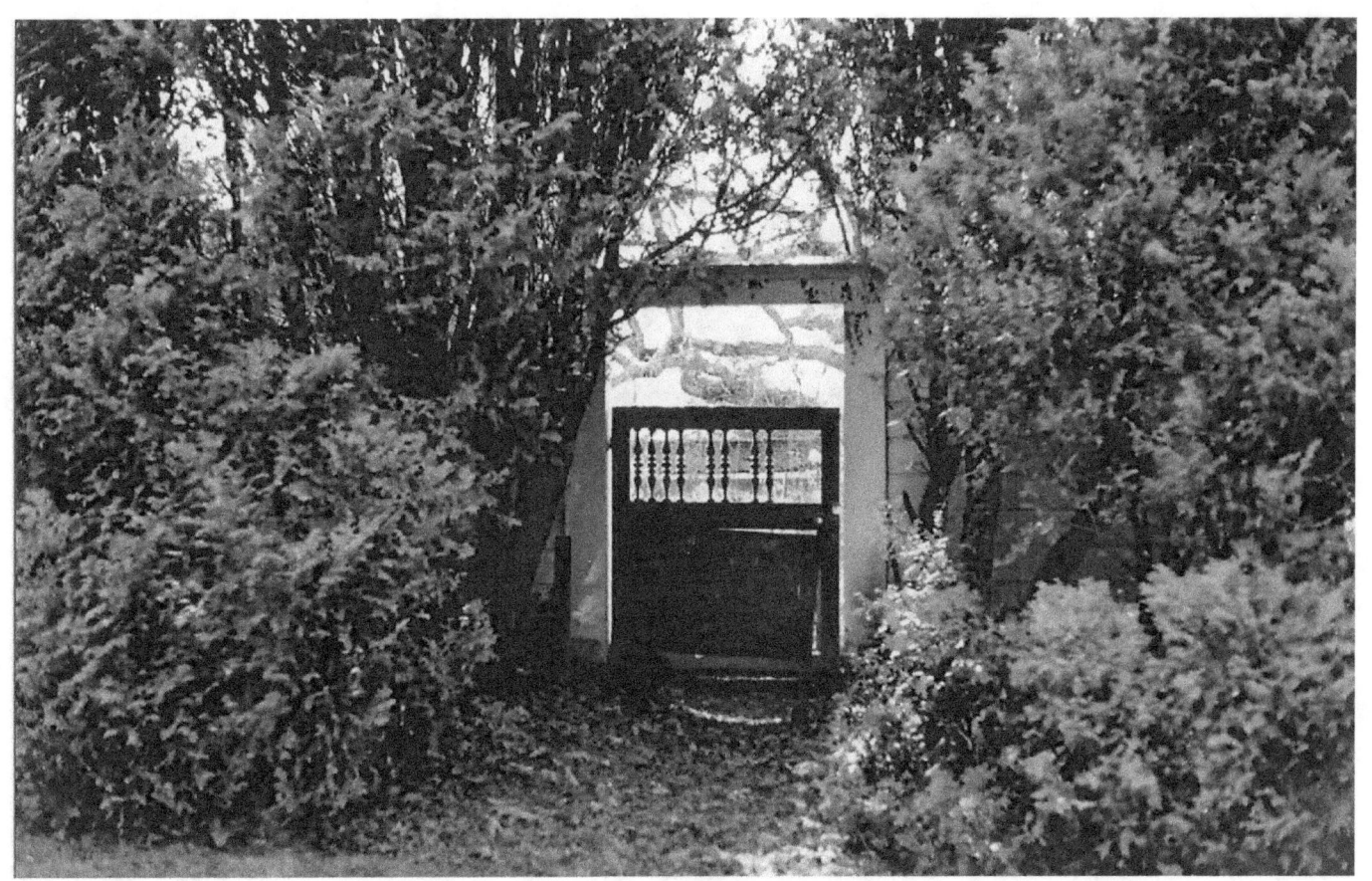

Gate to the garden

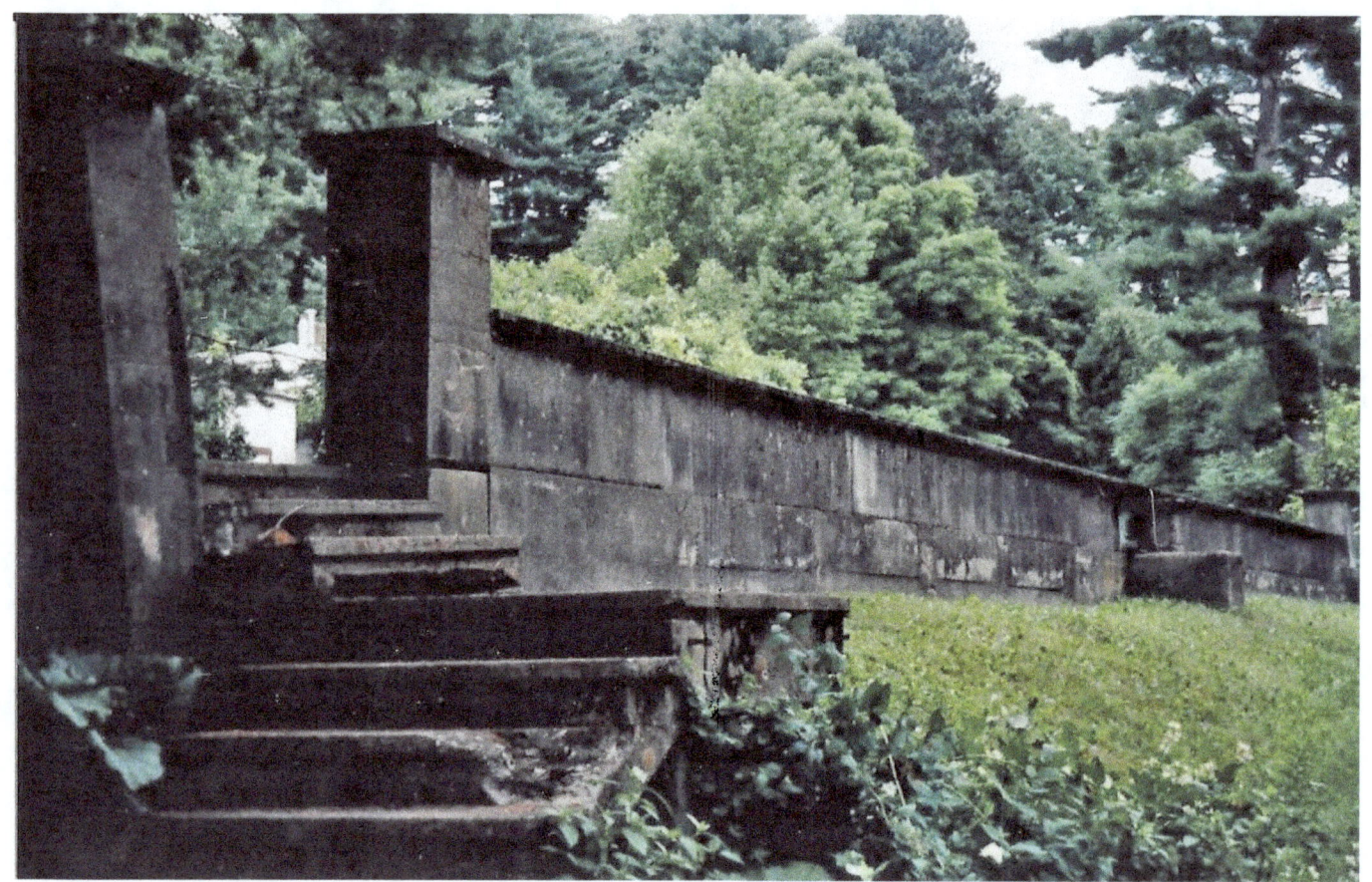

Mason walls and steps

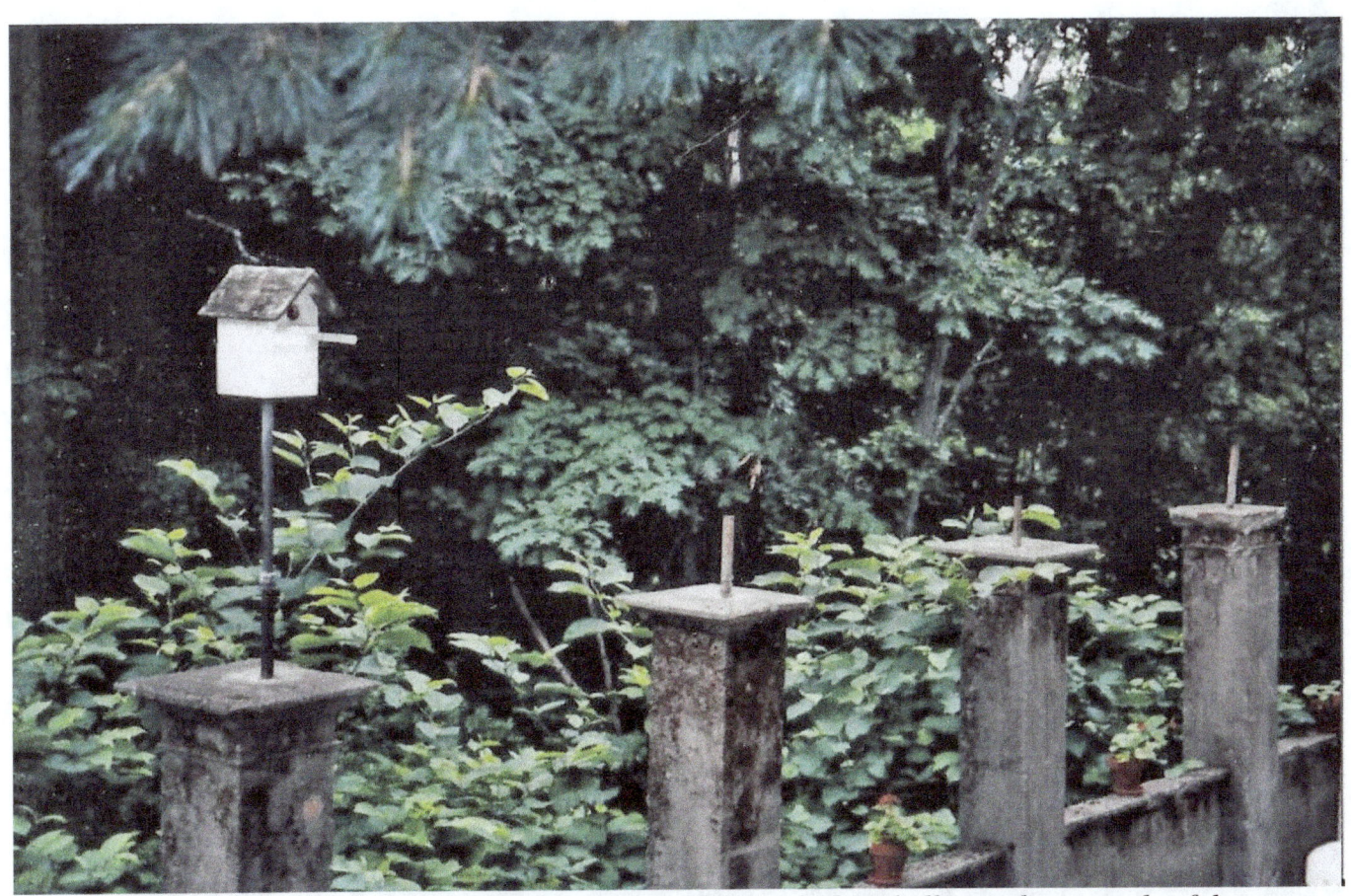

An example of the many birdhouses built by Maxfield Parrish, found all over the grounds of the estate.

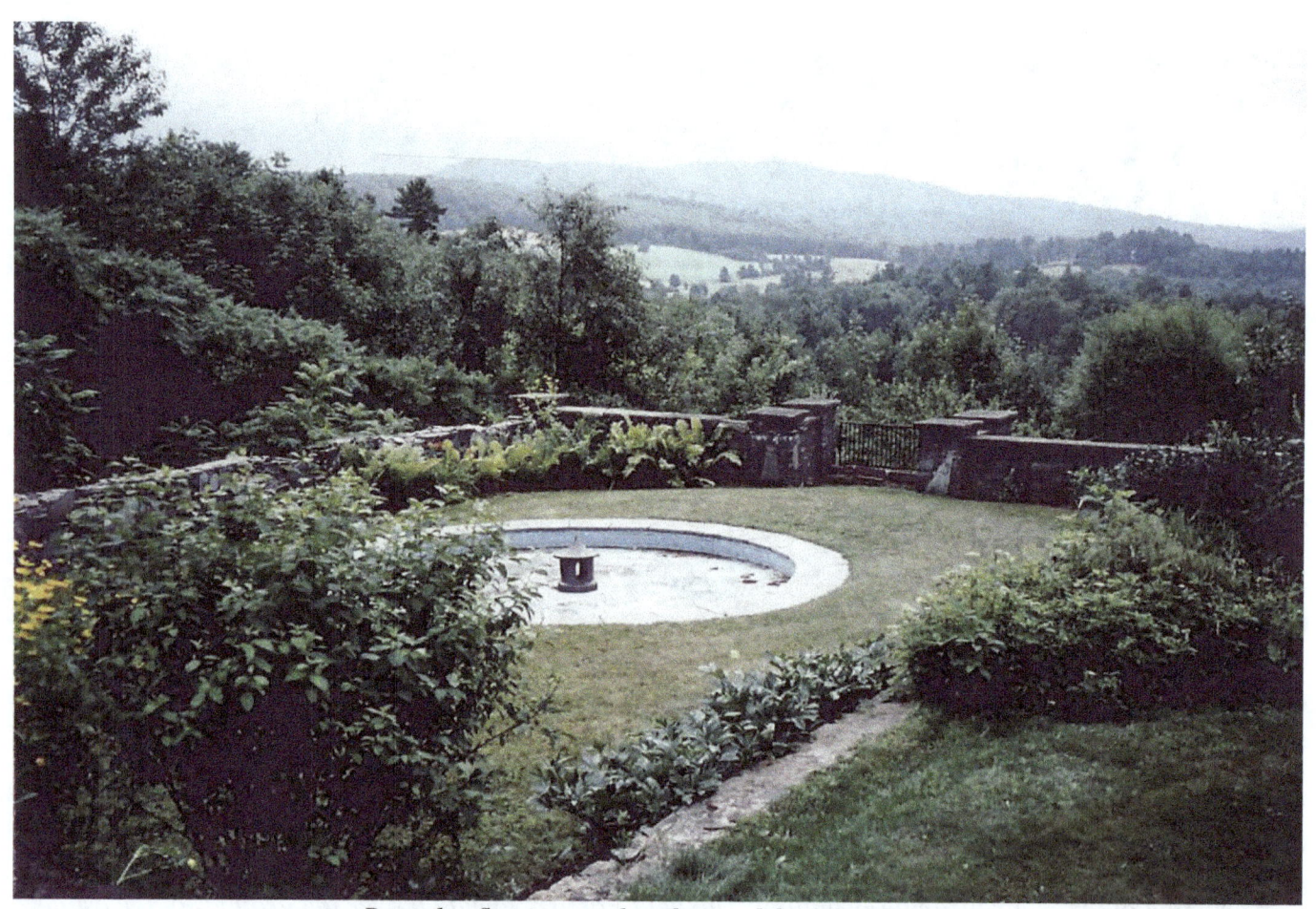

Round reflecting pool in front of the main house

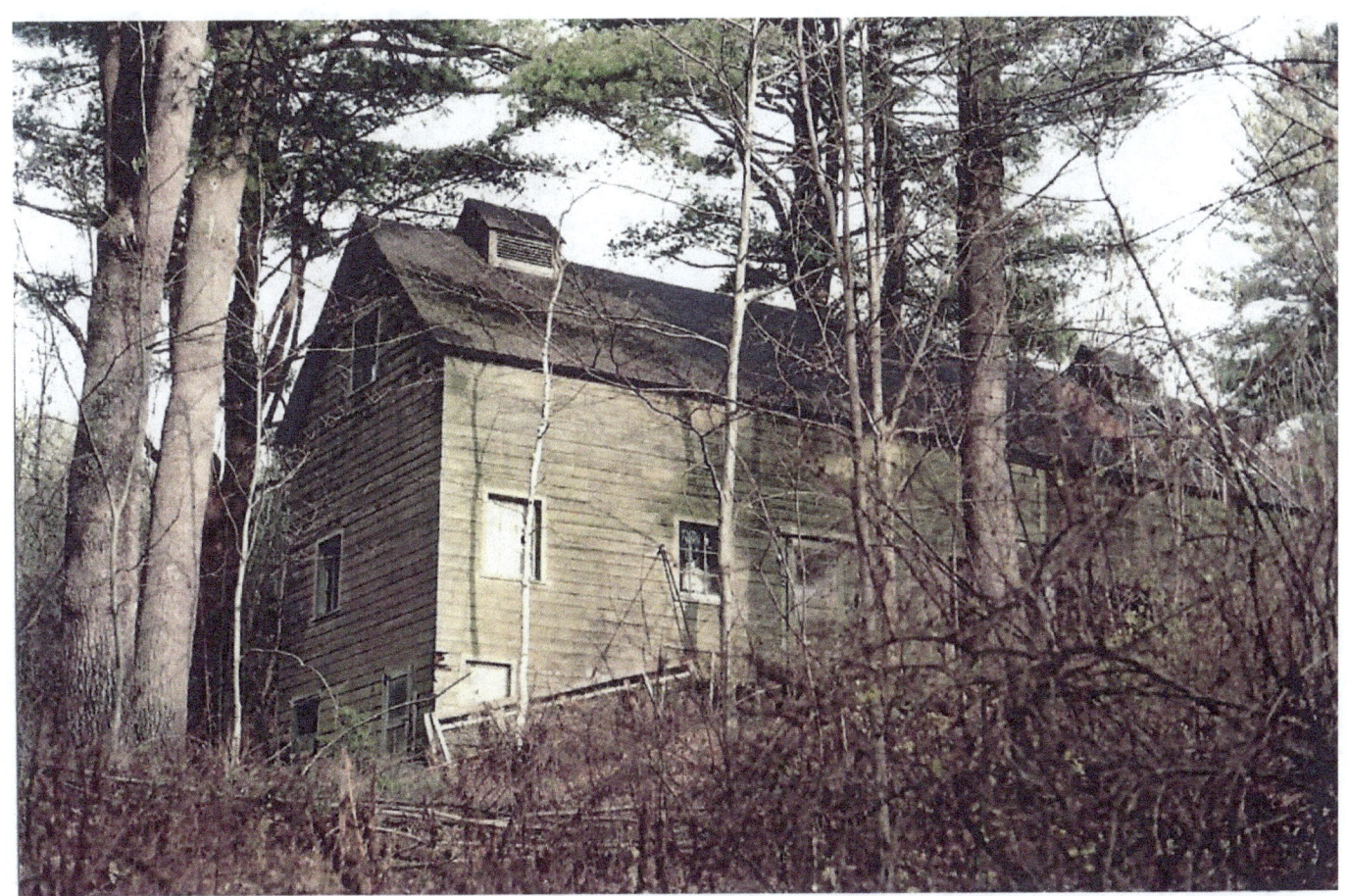

View of the back of the carriage house

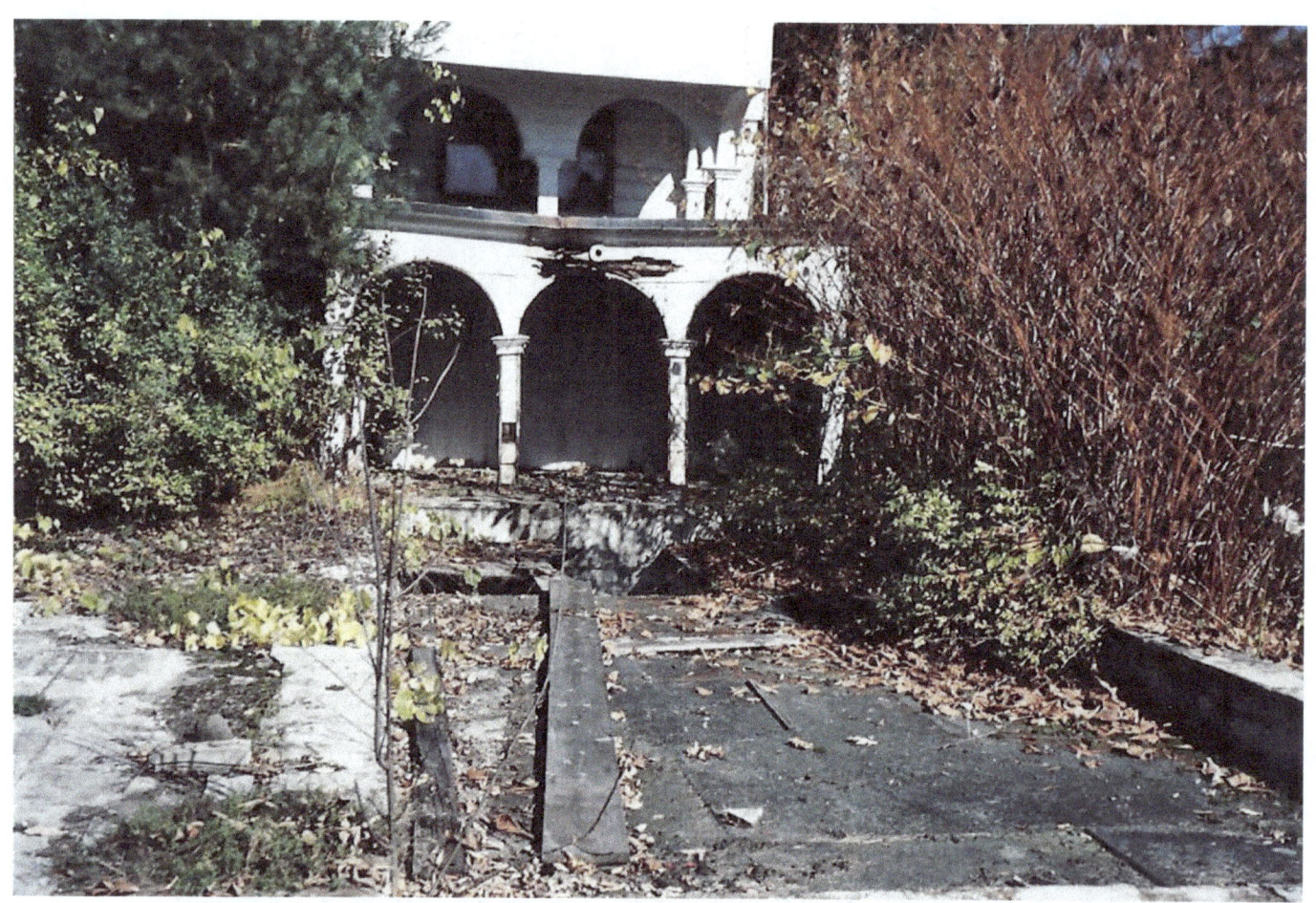

The triple archway and reflecting pool found in so many Parrish paintings.

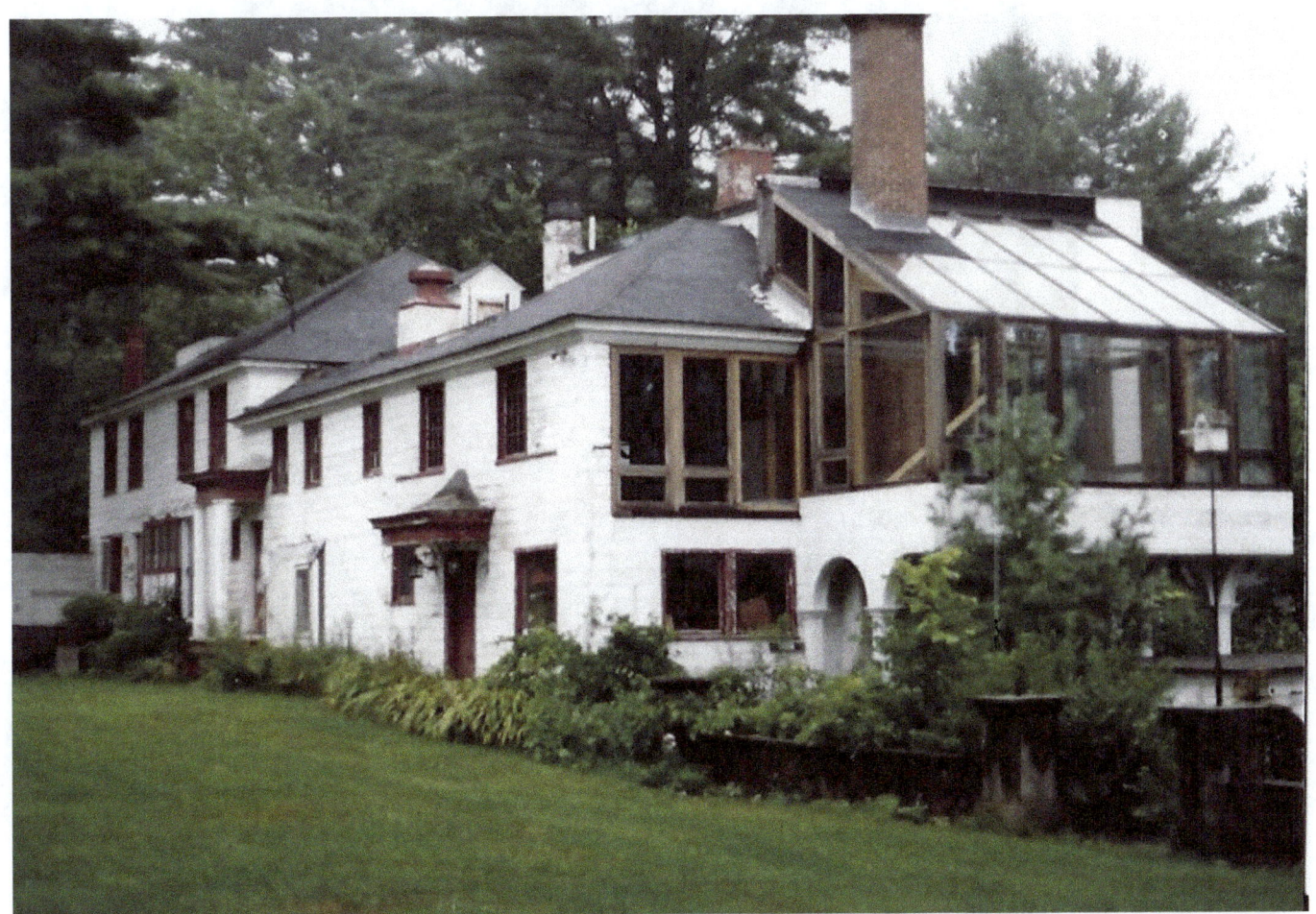

The art studio at the beginning of the demise—with many rooms, secret passageways and fireplaces. Note the famous white columns below on the right (from "Daybreak")--as you pass them, you would see the triple archway wand reflecting pool and many examples of his birdhouses.

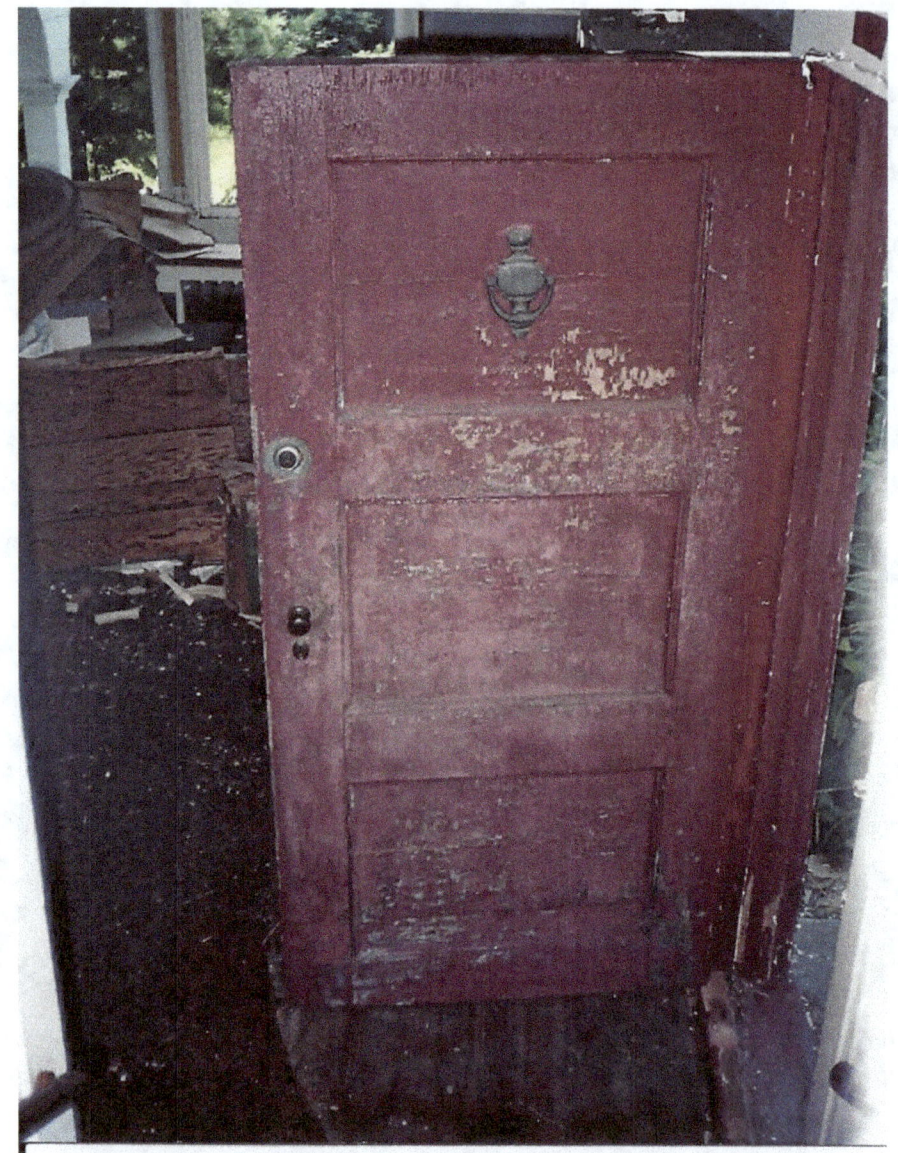

Red door to the studio

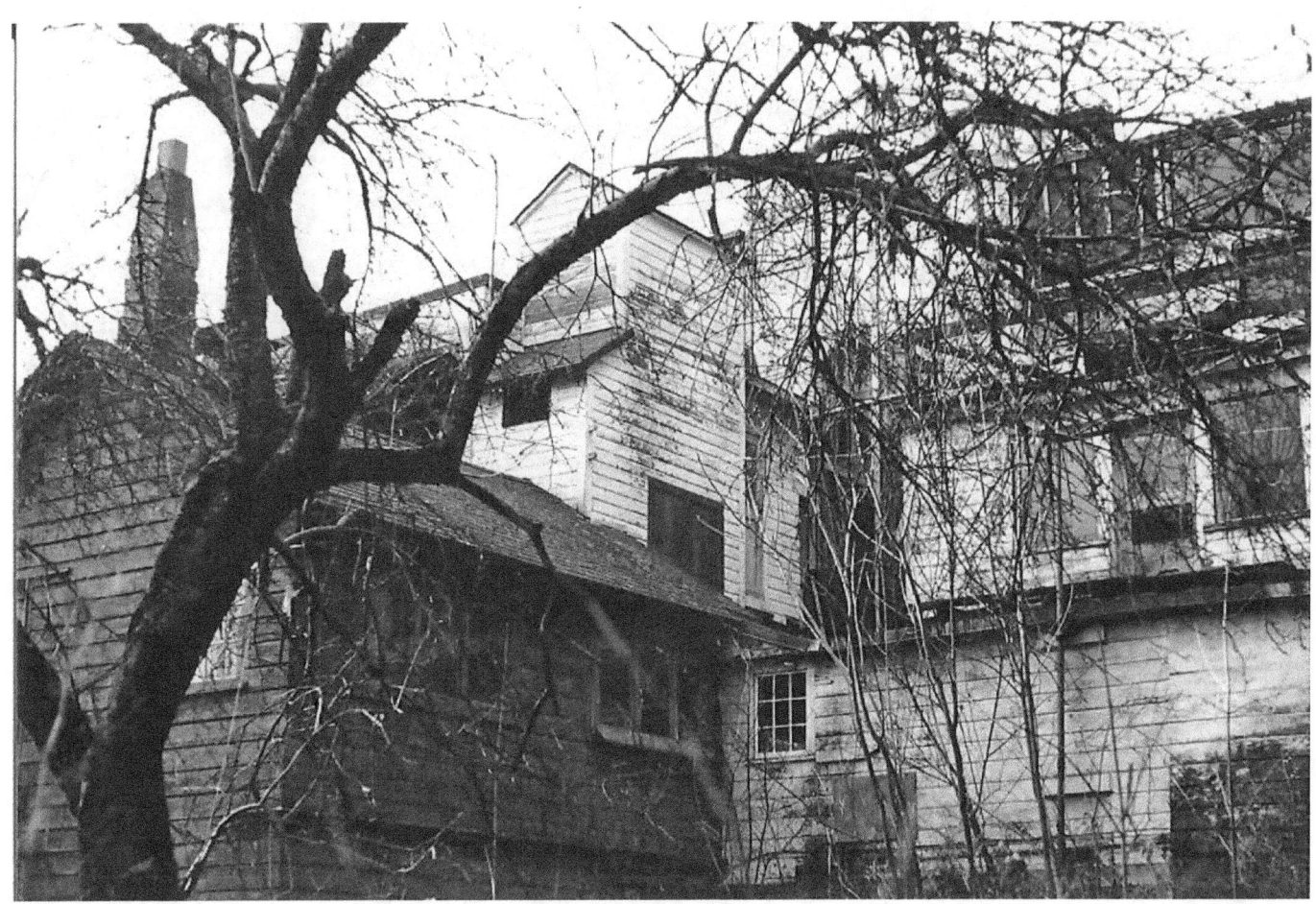

Rear of the art studio

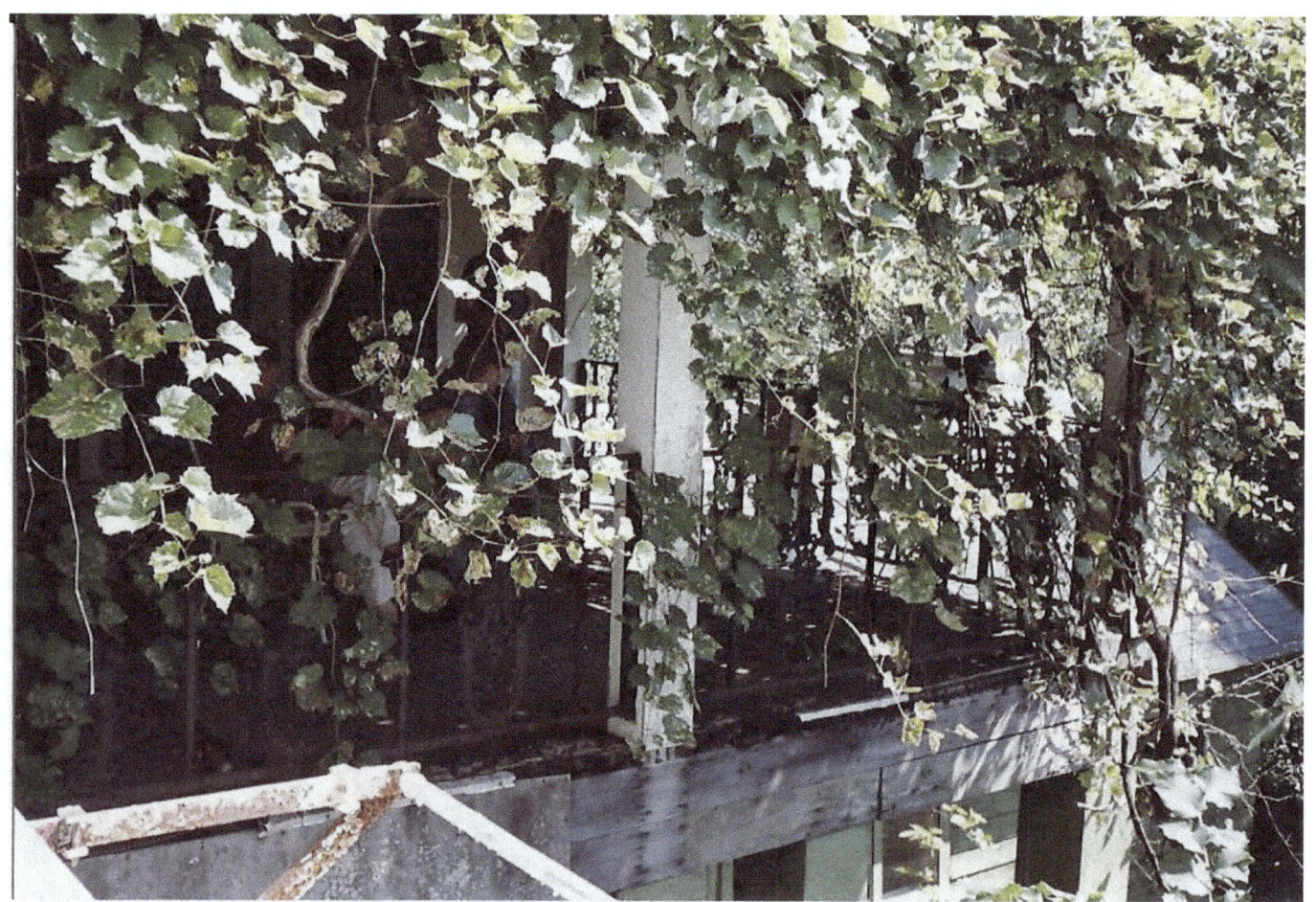

This is the vine-encased balcony porch where Maxfield Parrish would rest, take tea, and find inspiration. From here are many views used in his paintings.

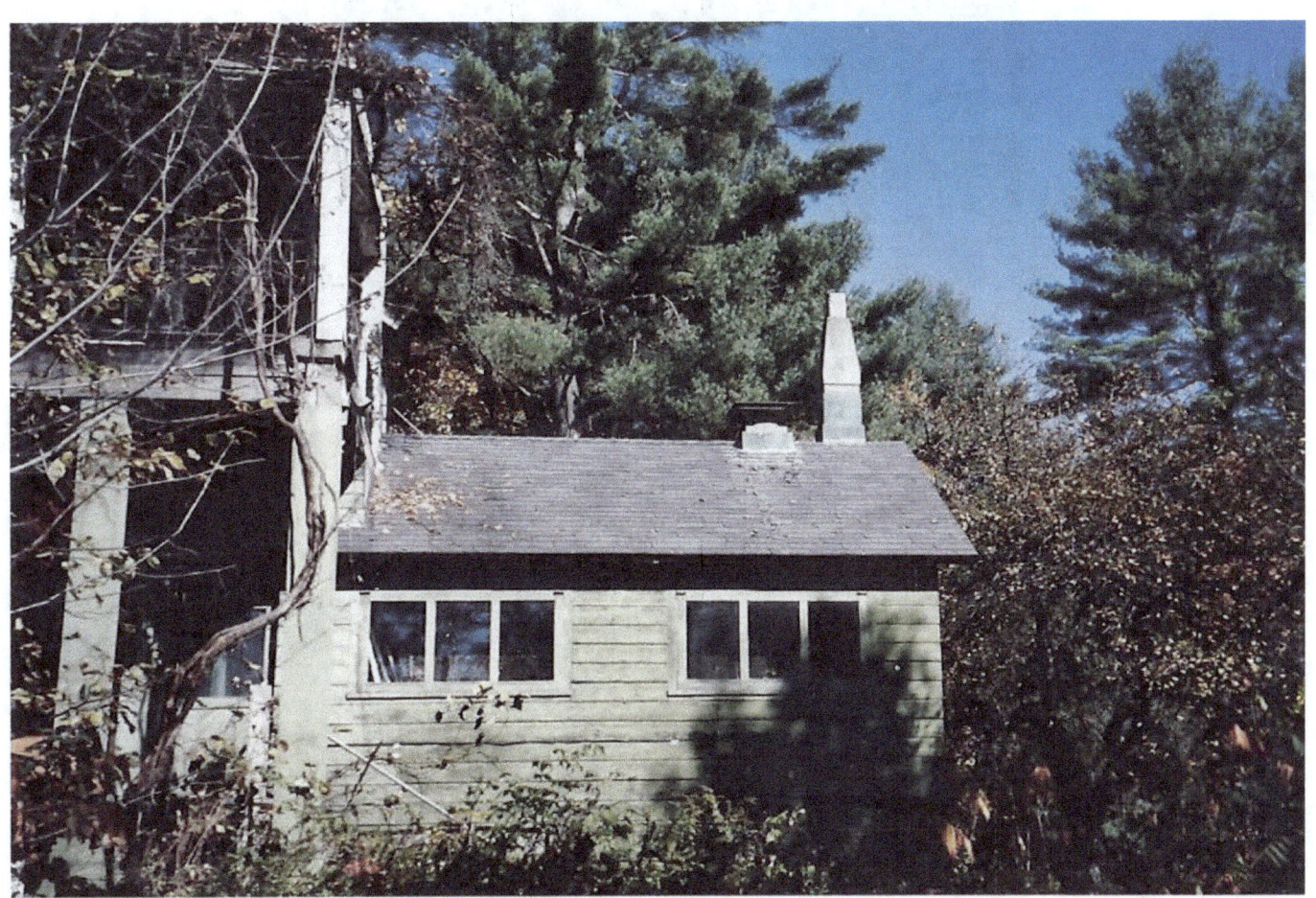

Birdbath on the roof of the building abutting the studio

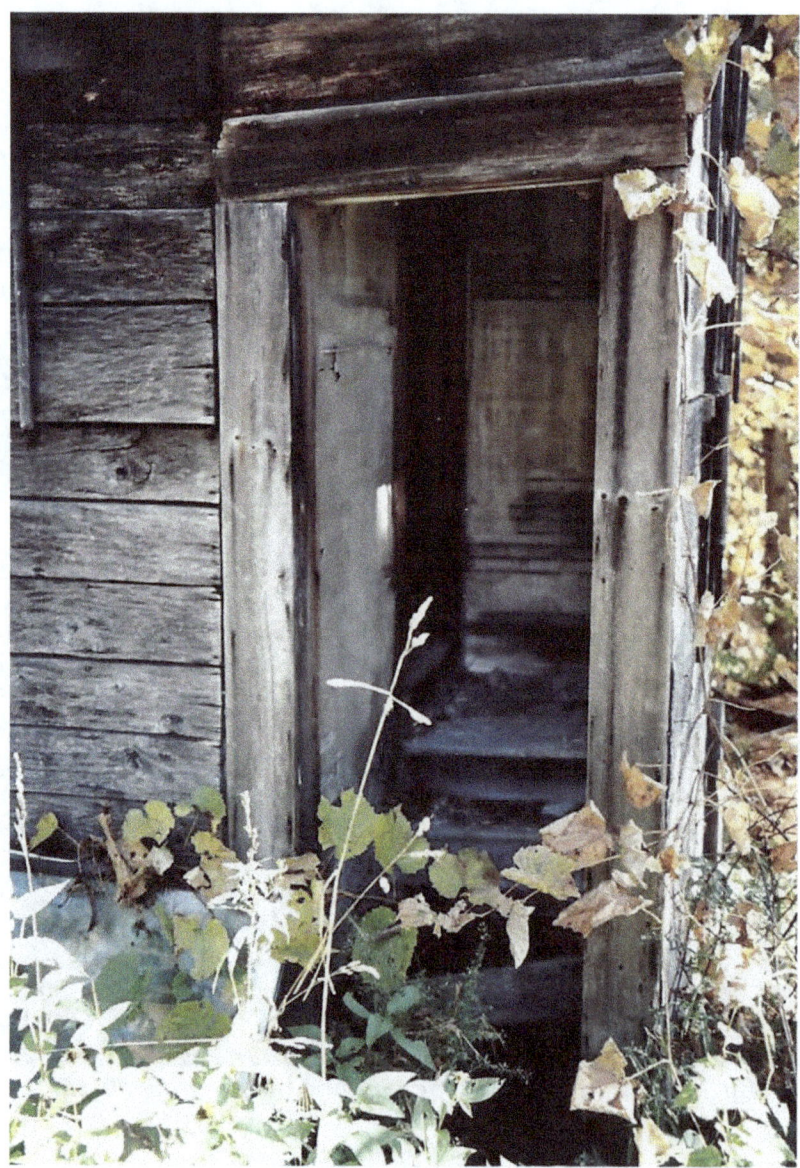

Two-seater outhouse entrance, next to Maxfield's mural room at the end of his studio.

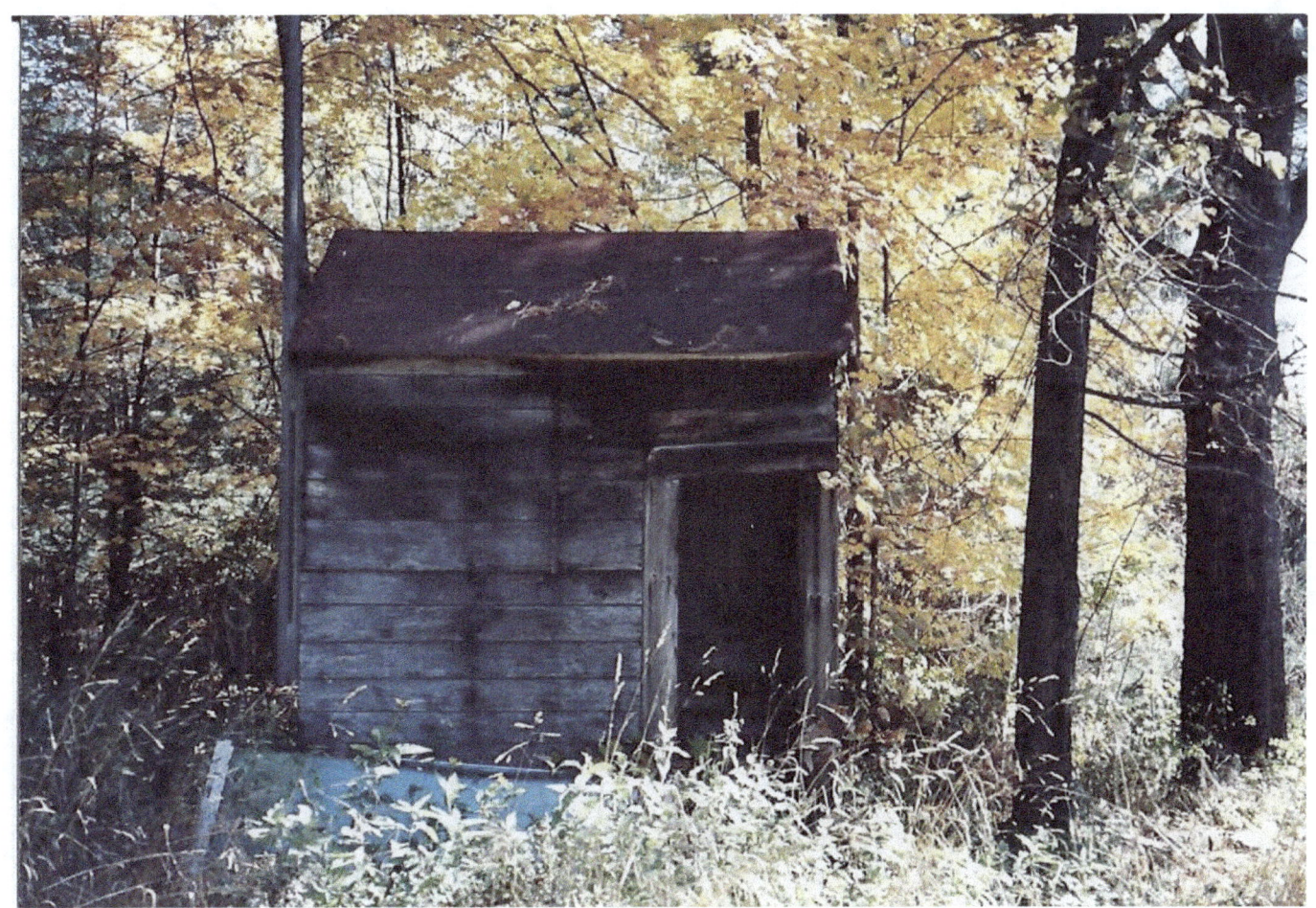

Parrish's outhouse

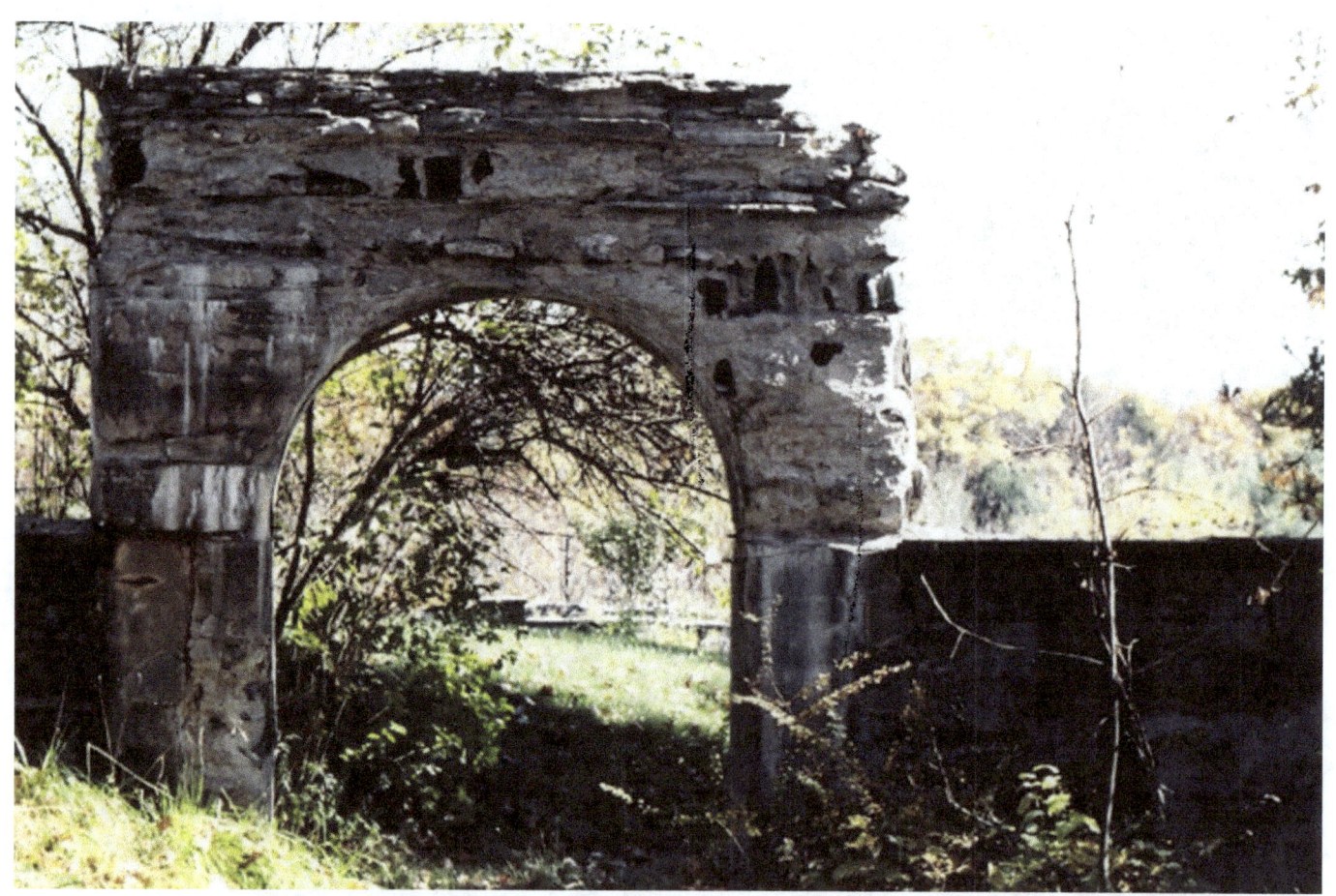

Archway in the gardens imbedded with wine bottles, since removed

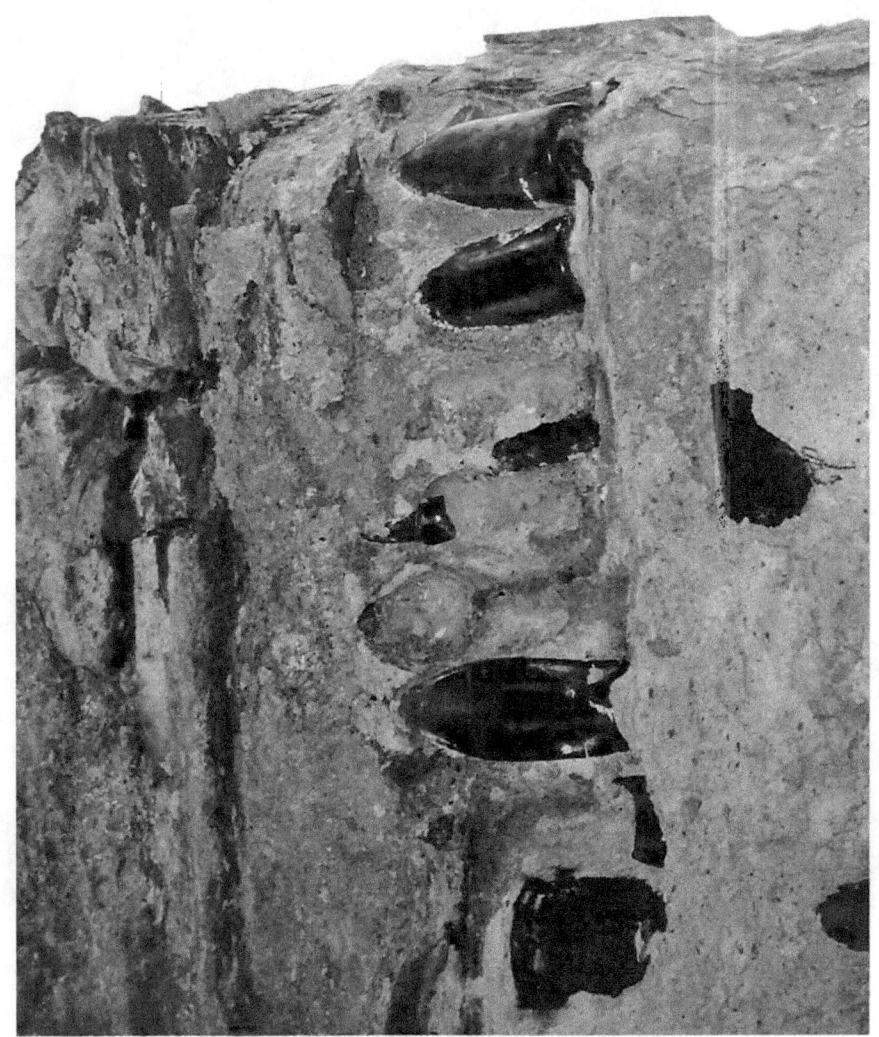

Closeup of the wine bottles in the archway

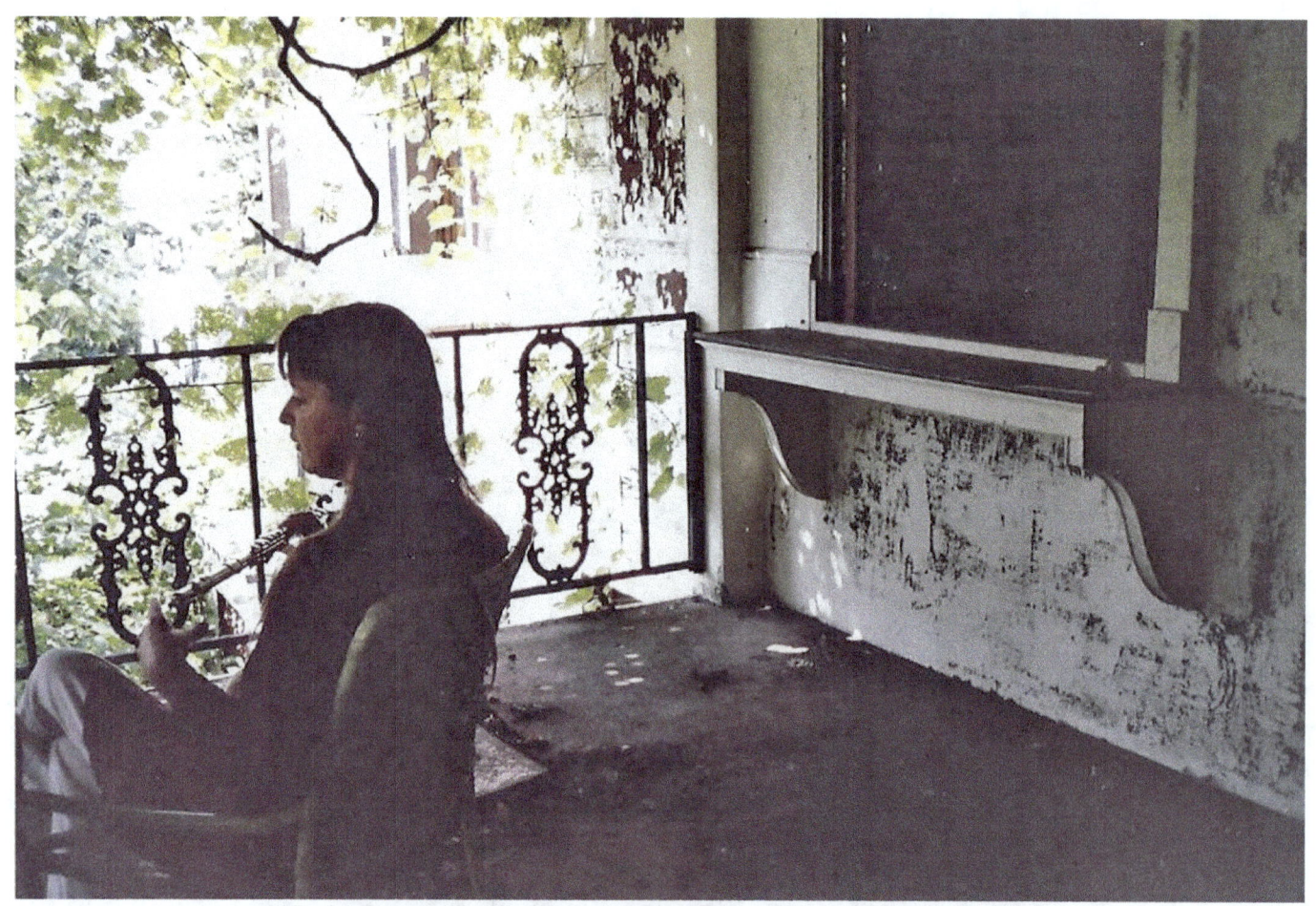

Robin recording as she plays her flute on the balcony porch

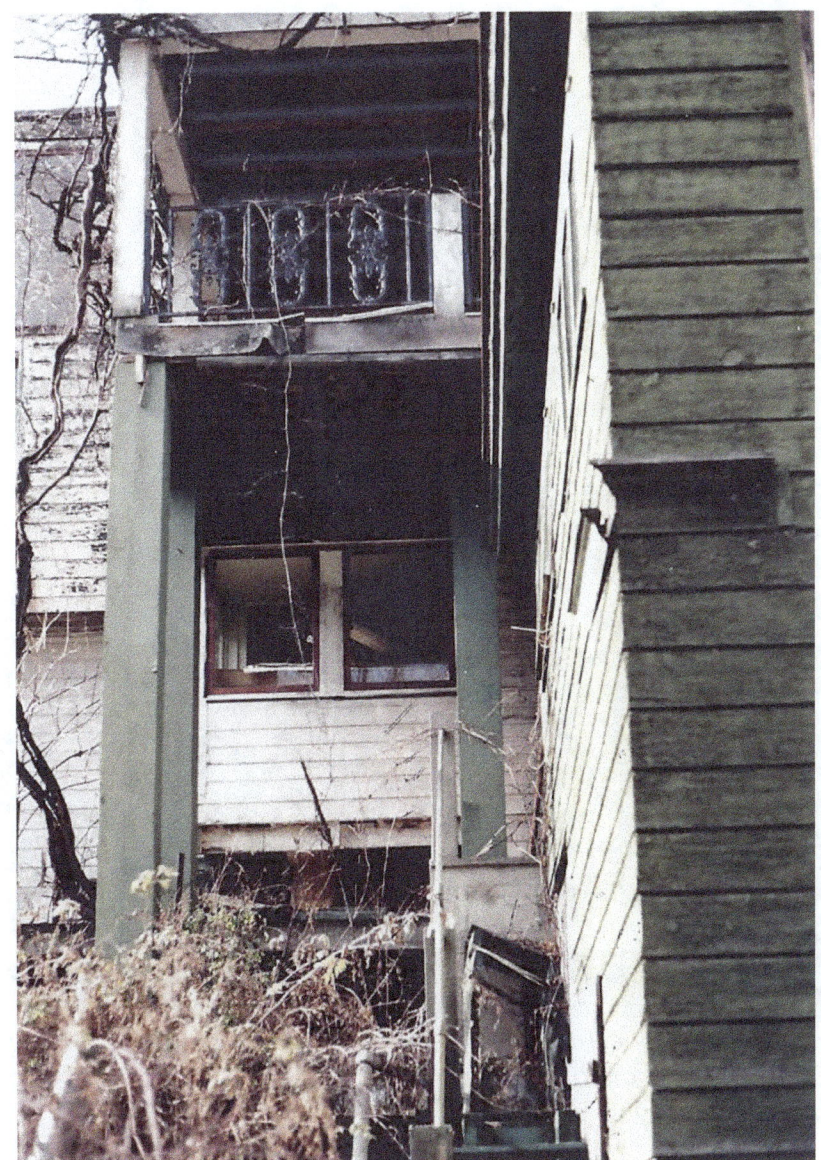

Balcony porch as seen from below

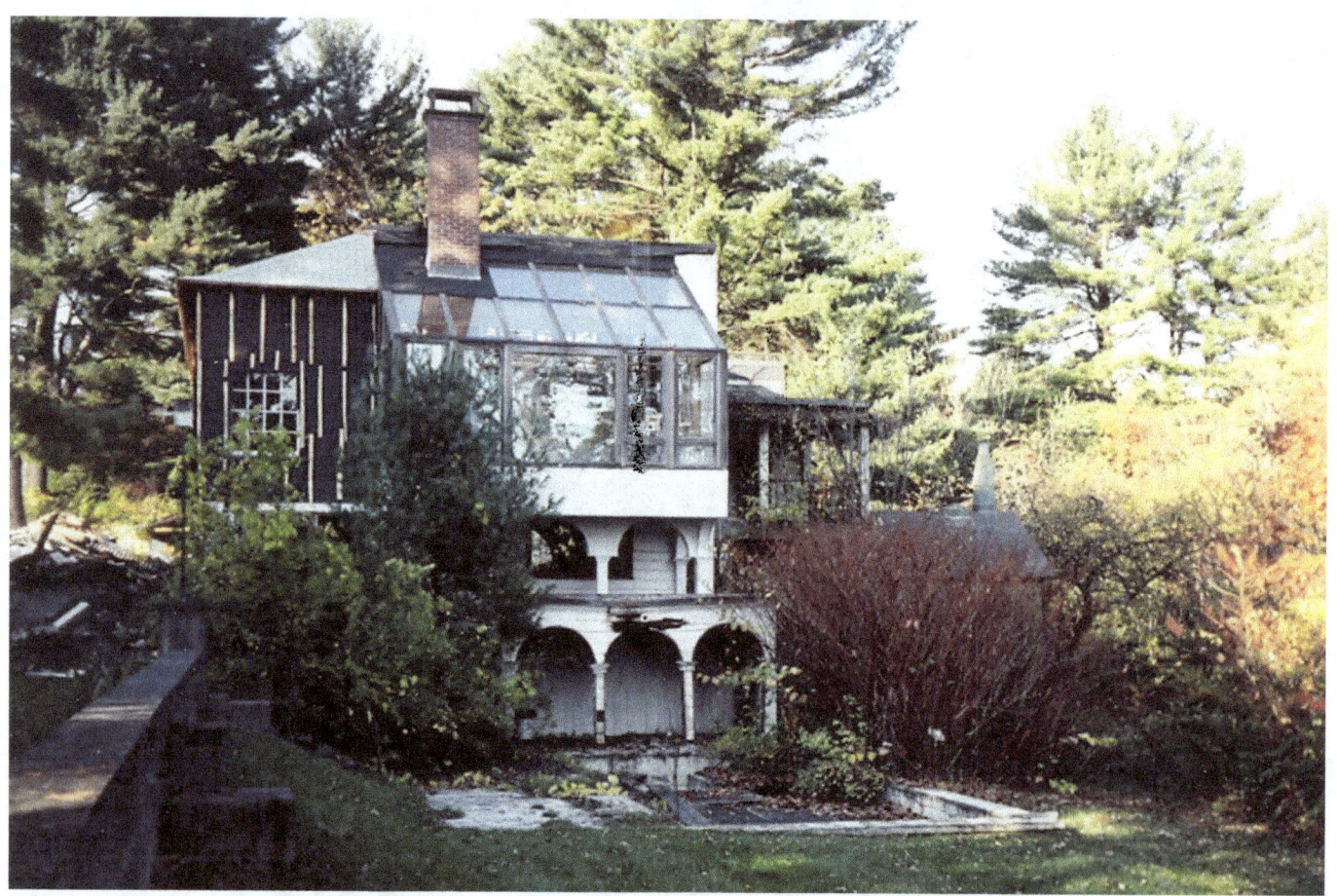

View of the triple archway and reflecting pool present in so many paintings. Note the tearing-down of the front of the workshop.

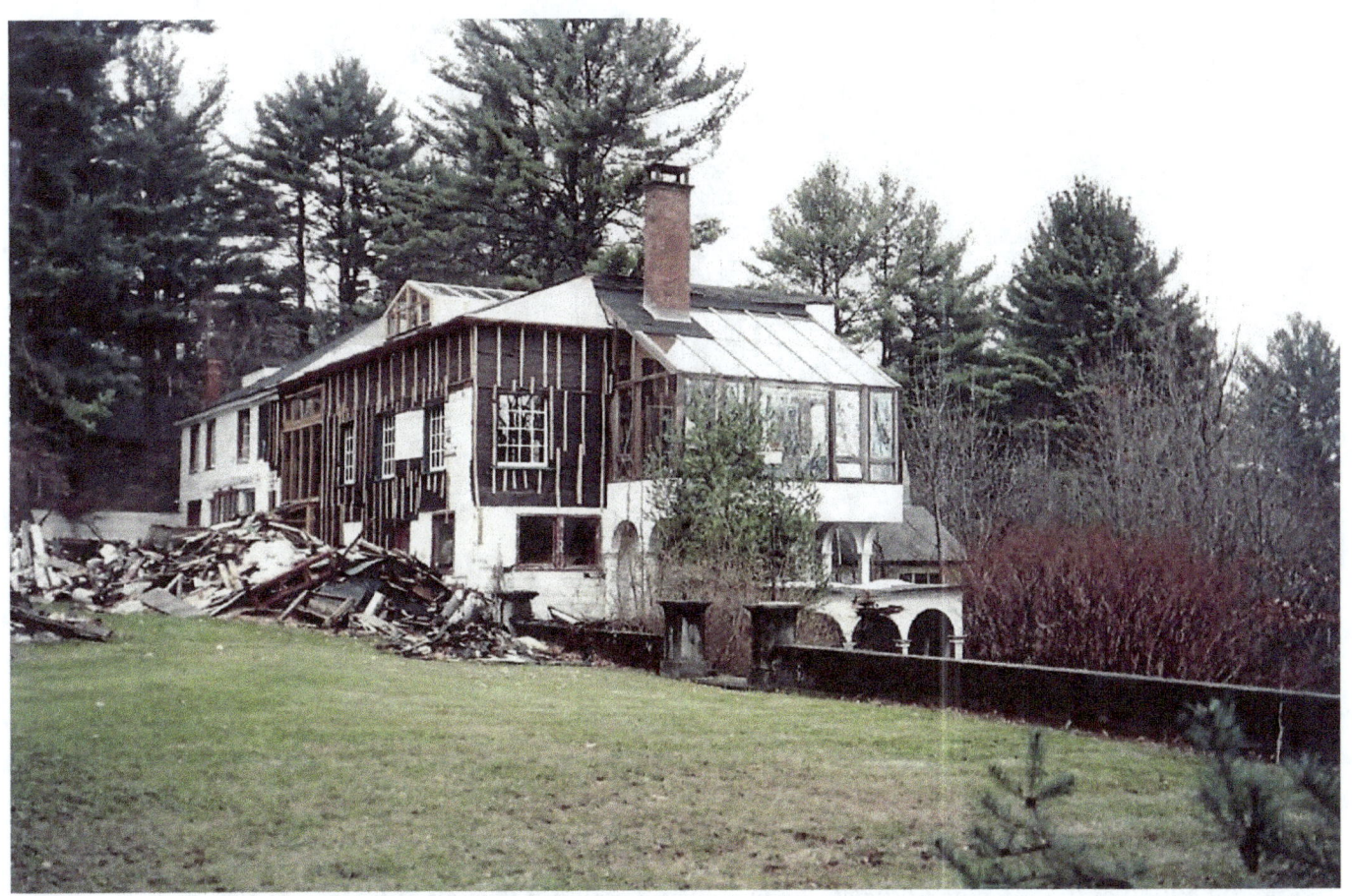

Demise of the art studio ... it could have been restored ... fortress in distress ... now I understand the whispers ... I understand it all ... "sanctuary dishonored"

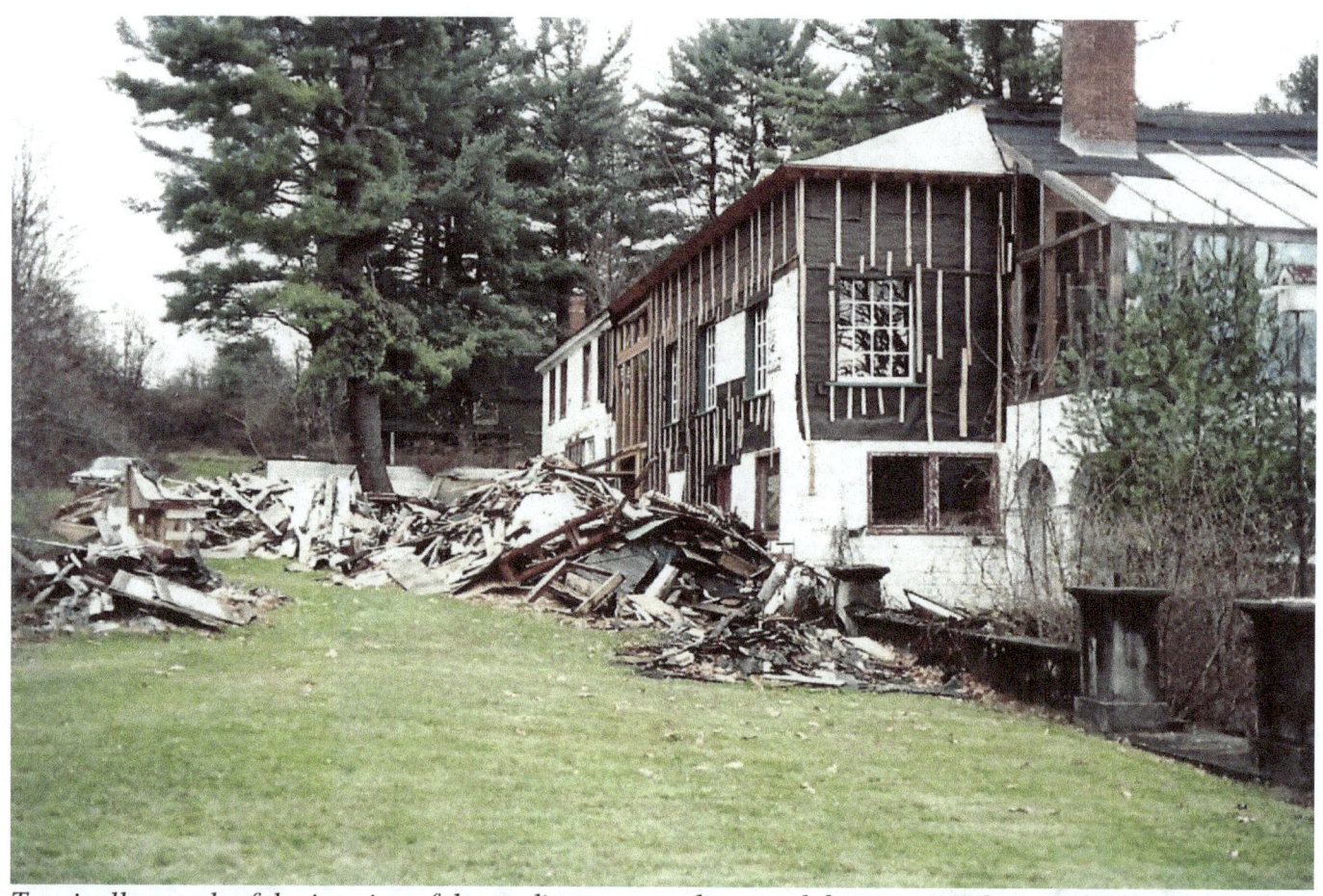

Tragically, much of the interior of the studio was torn down and thrown outside onto the lawn. Materials from the front of the studio were added to the pile. There was so much handmade artwork by Parrish on the inside. It was a masterpiece! This was his "belle of the ball" - his estate art studio.

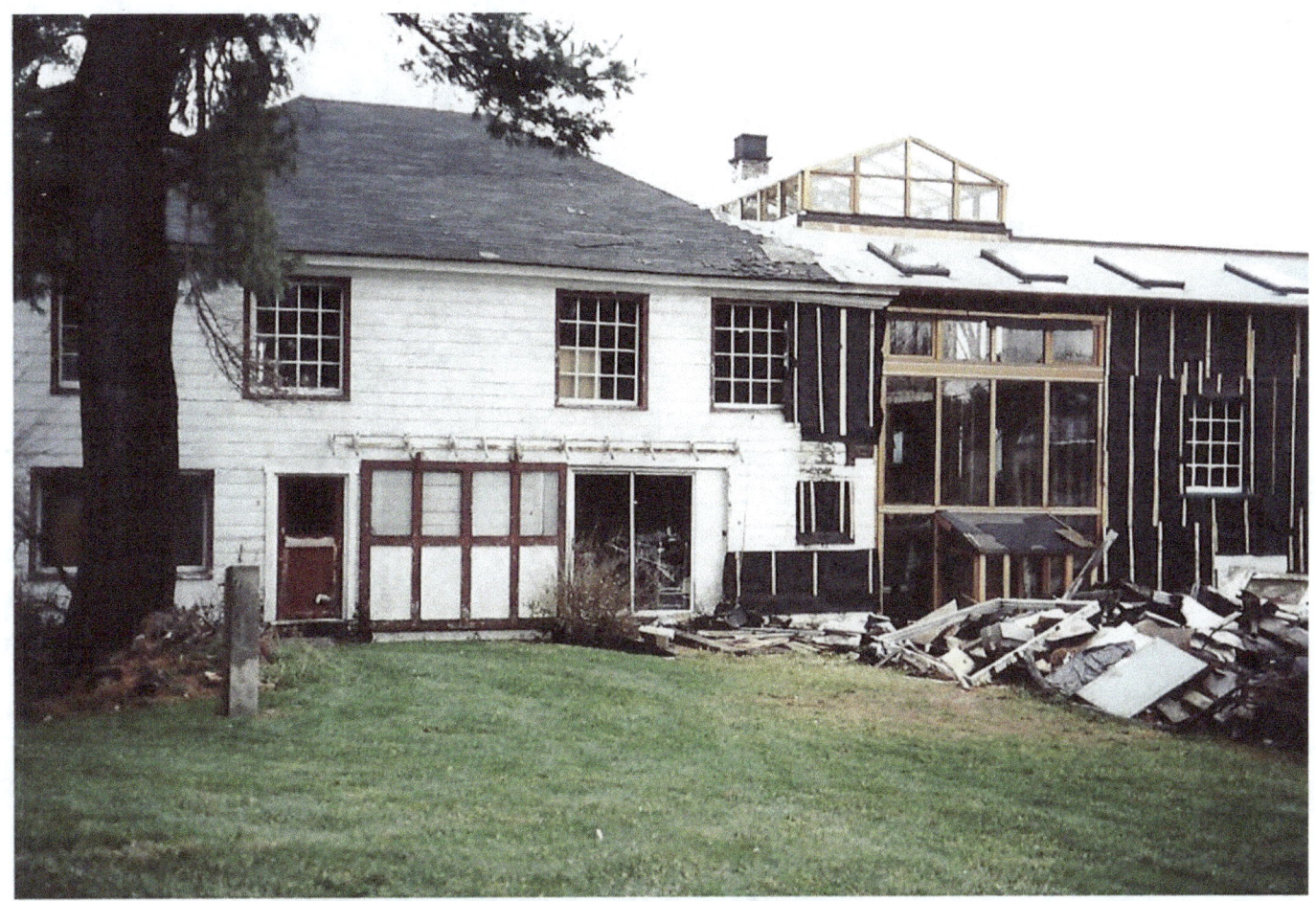

This section, where he created so many of his famous large panels and murals, was next to be demolished. Hidden stairways and secret passages were throughout the studio.

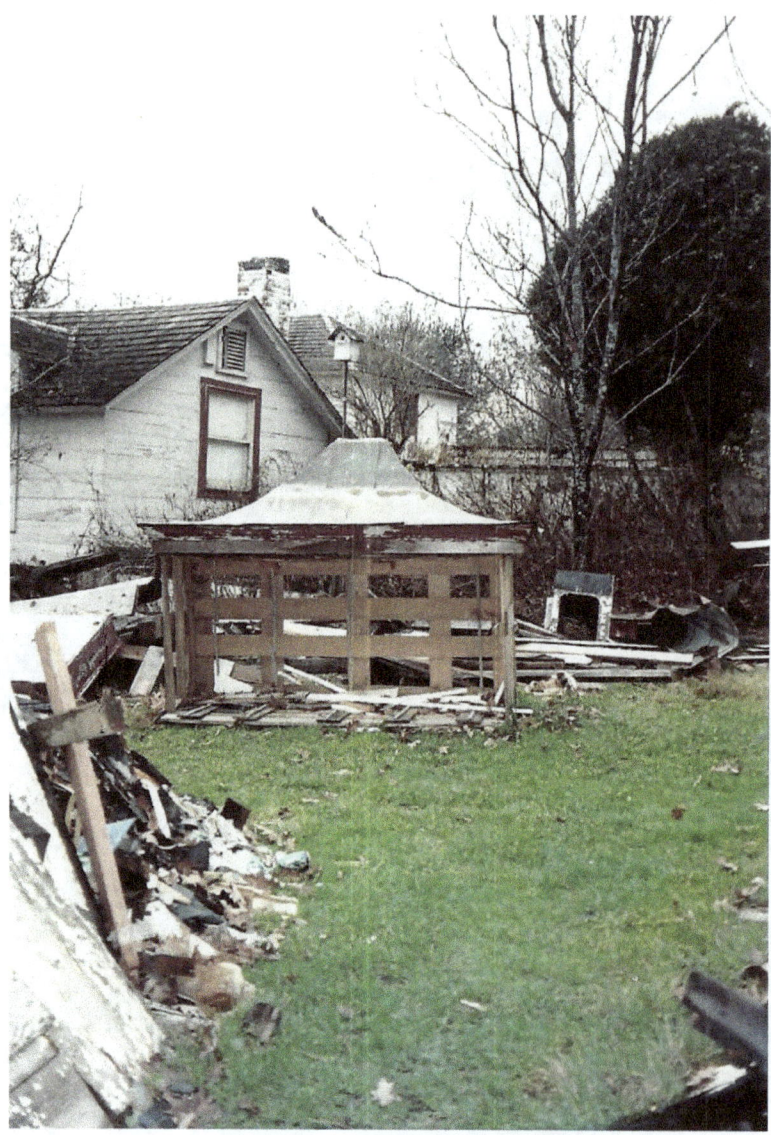

The little copper roof is ruined! Another birdhouse can be seen in the background.

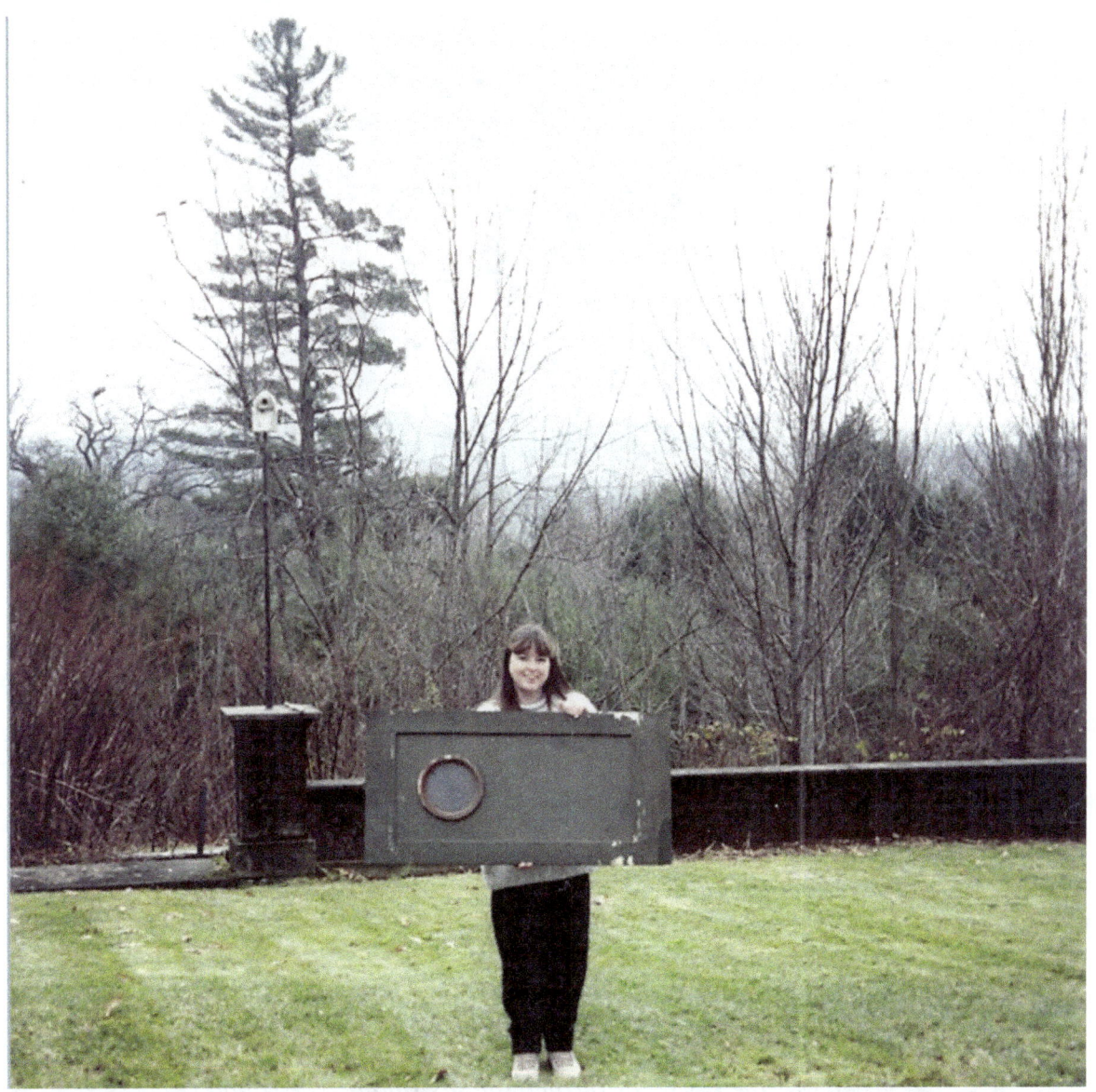

The author holding a panel given to her by her hostess. The tree in the background is the one remaining from a pair of trees found in many Parrish masterpieces. One tree was struck by lightning and died. Parrish put a lightning rod on this one.

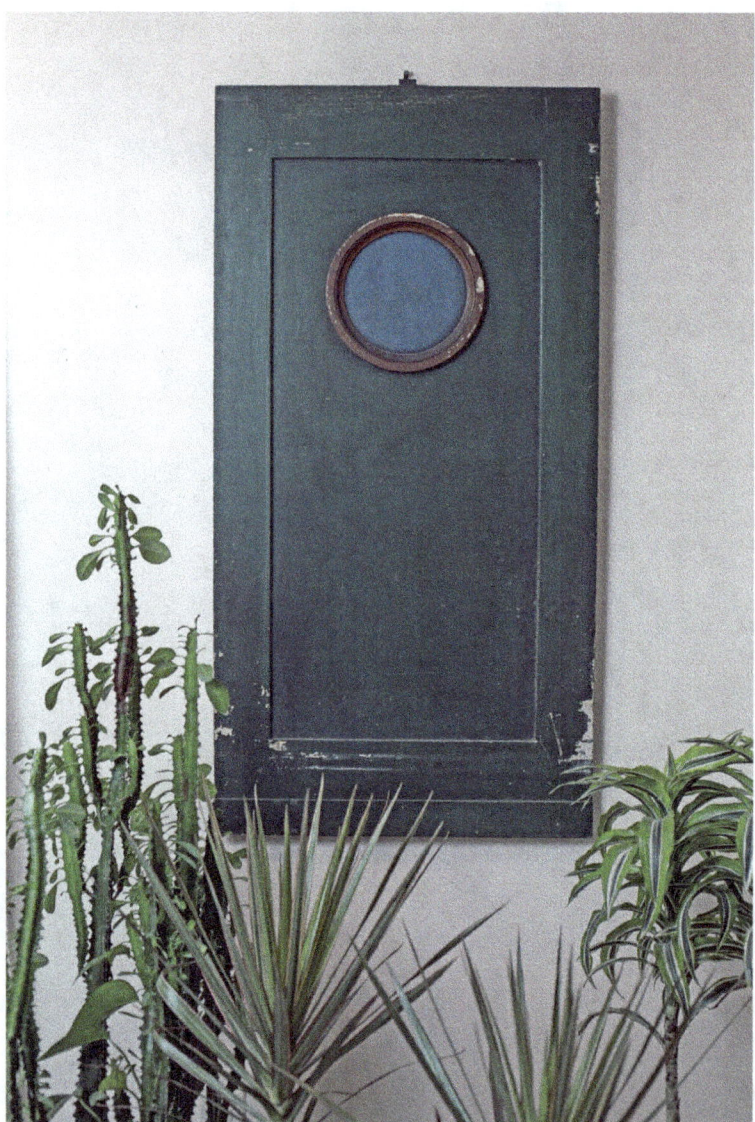

*This panel is as found – all original paint. The deep
green was the key color throughout his studio. The round
motif, it's deep blue and colorful ring, were found all
over. My film footage shows this green everywhere – it
seemed to be his favorite color.*

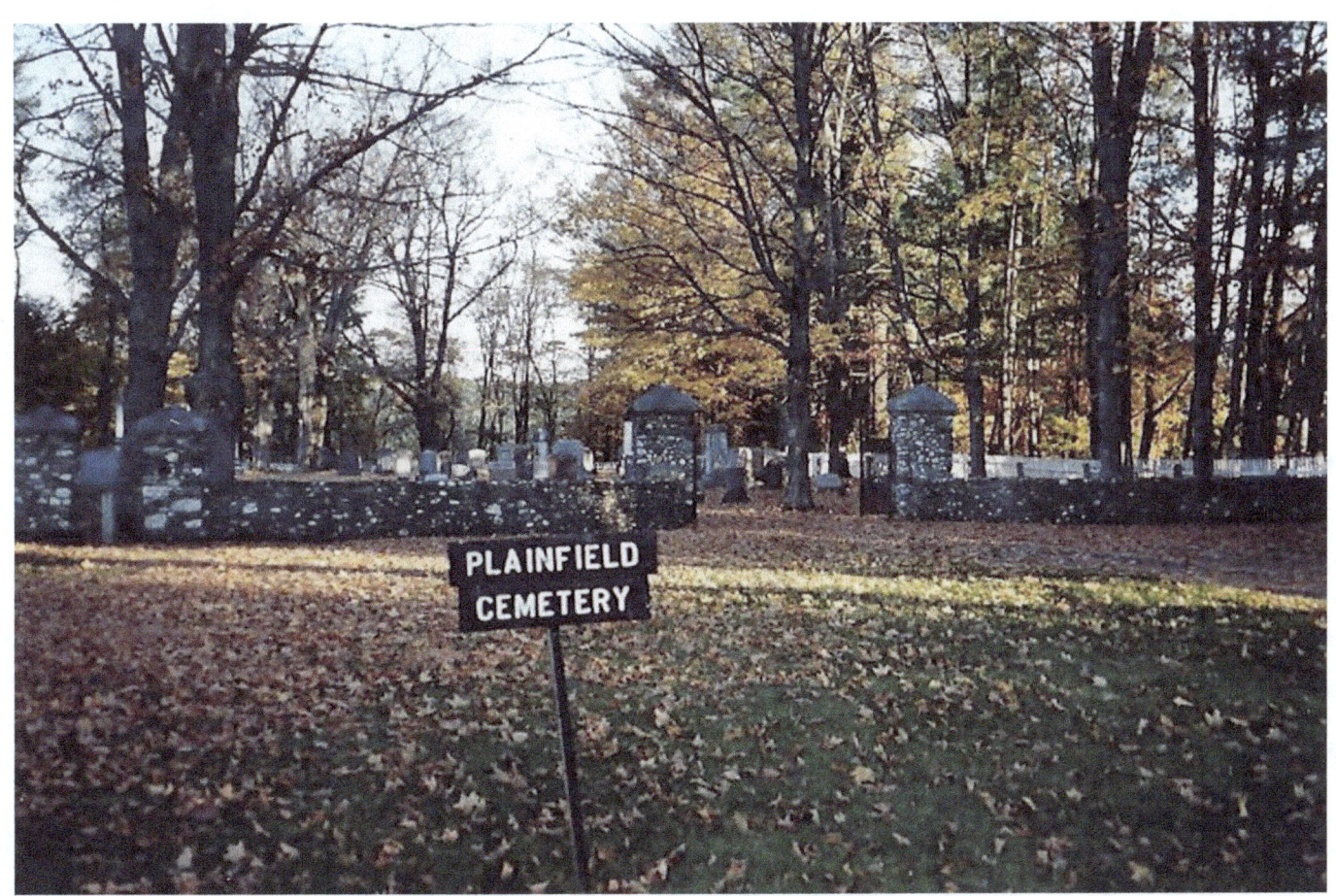

Entrance to the Plainfield Cemetery

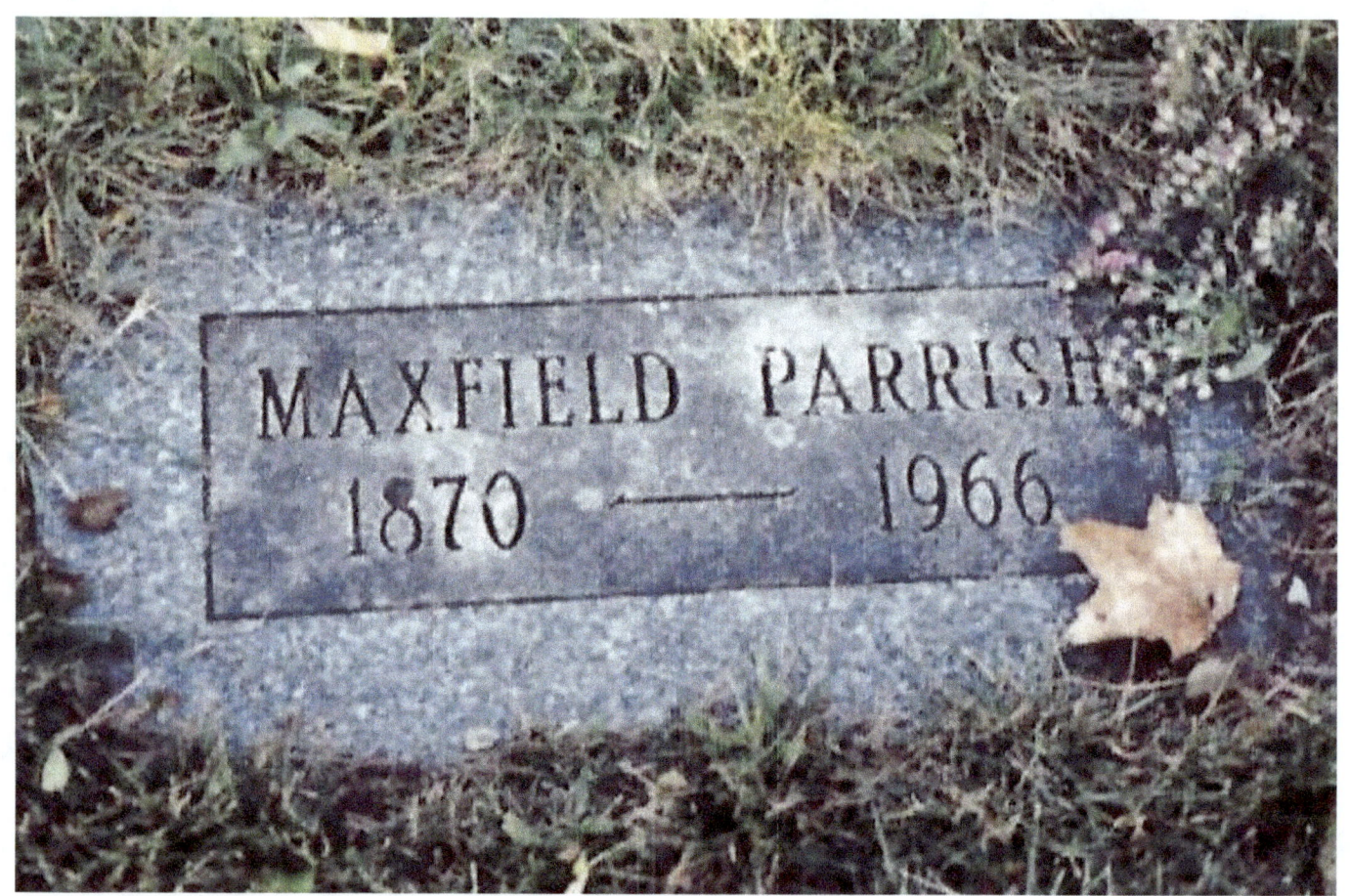

Maxfield Parrish's headstone

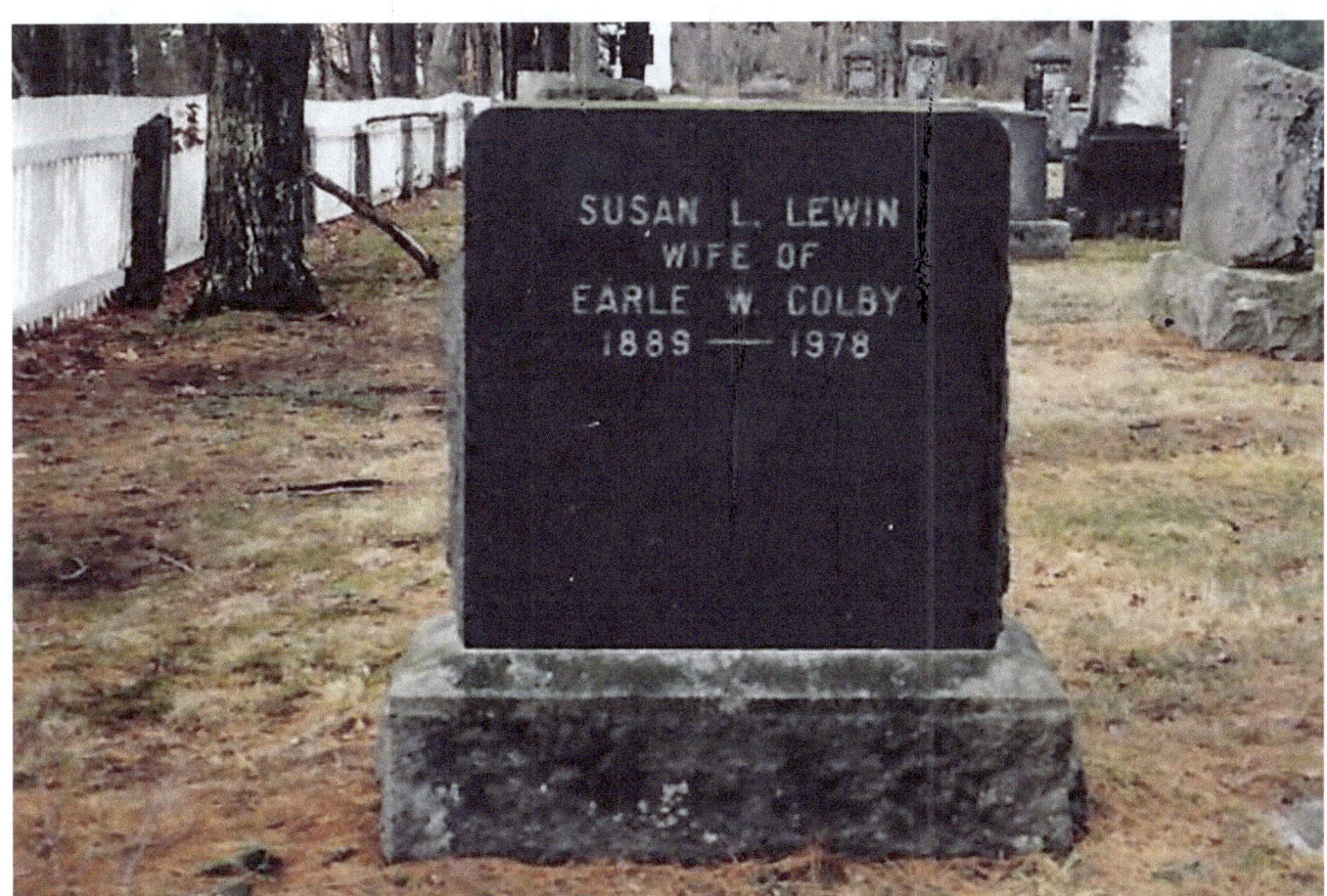

Grave of Sue Lewin, just a "stone's throw" away from Parrish's grave.

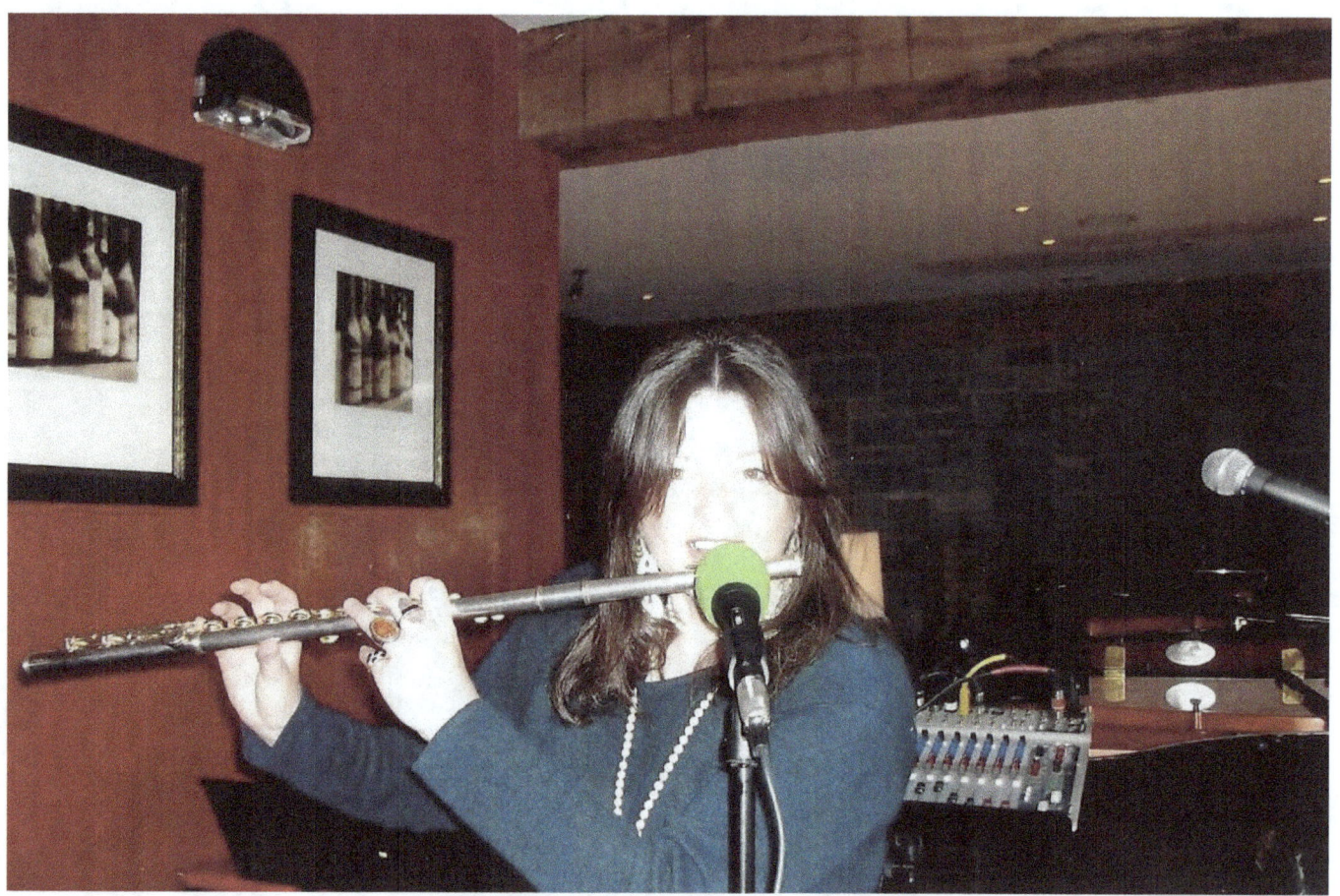

Author Robin Lee (Photo by Brenda)

Closing Remarks

A turn of events in my personal life have guided me to reopen my Maxfield Parrish story I have kept under lock and key for over twenty years. Whispers have a way of returning and advising and the time finally seems right to unveil my project. Years of intense research of Parrish regarding my film footage and exchanges with experts have opened my eyes to who Maxfield Parrish really was.

I videoed Parrish's beloved estate and art studio at the exact moment in time when it was still somewhat intact, but about to be altered beyond recognition. I was certainly there for a reason—to document all I could about this historic landmark—The Oaks.

I videoed his inner sanctuary, the bedroom where he passed away, his theatrical living room with the Juliet balcony and his stately fireplace.

The sweeping views of his property were a well-spring of inspirations for this master artist. I recorded his private office where many of his intriguing round motifs were displayed—so many rooms with secret passageways, trapdoors and artwork painted on the ceiling. It was endless! All of these precious rooms, steeped in art history, were once private and kept from the world. A creative genius lived and worked here. His world famous masterpieces were born here in this magnificent and iconic studio.

We are working on other books to come, and a most incredible movie on Parrish and Sue Lewin. This movie is based on information handed down and will expose the truth about Parrish and his faithful friend and servant—Sue Lewin. Art history and a timeless love story will emerge.

In the fall of 2012, I met up with another filmer, a documentarian, at the local film festival. I had been searching for the perfect partner in my quest. He was blown away by the film footage at the Parrish estate and my story. He has become a vital companion, helping me to document everything—part of the team that has coalesced to venture wherever this will take us.

I have vital and important documentation of Parrish's true artwork and life. Bit by bit, we will release all of this as we go along. Stay tuned!

--- Robin Lee

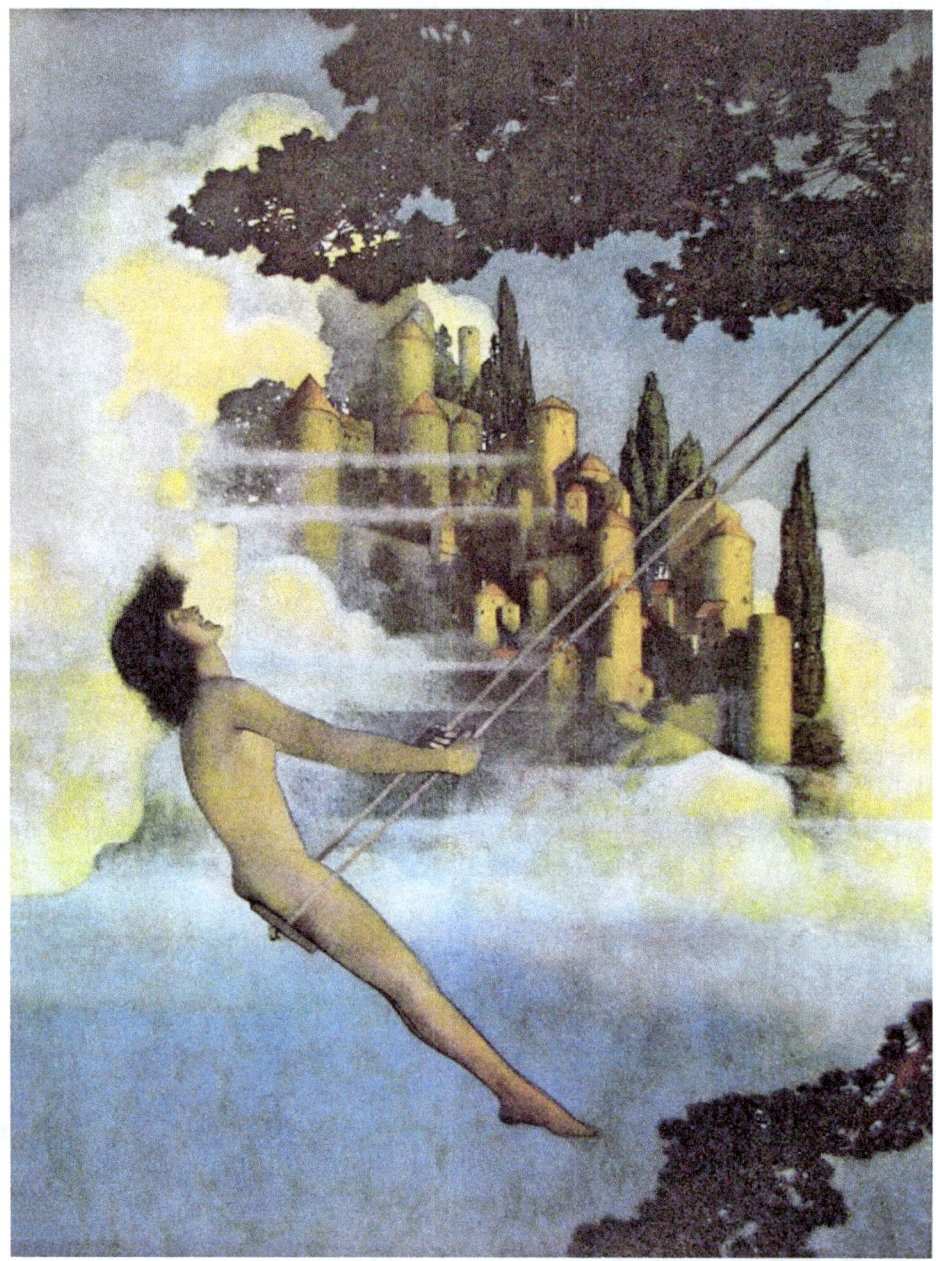

The Dinky Bird, *by Maxfield Parrish, an illustration from* Poems of Childhood *by Eugene Field, 1904*.

www.ingramcontent.com/pod-product-compliance
Lightning Source LLC
Chambersburg PA
CBHW080401190526
45161CB00003B/96